Men Don't Run
In the Rain

Men Don't Run In the Rain

A Son's Reflections on Life, Faith, and an Iconic Father

By Rick Burgess

Published by Iron Hill Press

Published by:

Men Don't Run In the Rain: A Son's Reflections on Life, Faith, and an Iconic Father

©2025 by Rick Burgess. All rights reserved.

Published by Iron Hill Press in the United States of America.

Library of Congress Cataloging-in-Publication Data is on file at the Library of Congress, Washington, DC.

ISBN: 9798991329118

All rights reserved. The scanning, uploading, and electronic sharing of any part of this book without the publisher's permission, constitutes unlawful piracy and theft of the author's intellectual property. If you would like to use material from the book (other than for review purposes), prior written permission must be obtained by contacting the publisher at info@ironhillpress.com.

Unless otherwise noted, Scripture quotations are from the ESV® Bible (The Holy Bible, English Standard Version®), copyright © 2001 by Crossway, a publishing ministry of Good News Publishers. Used by permission. All rights reserved.

Cover Design: Faceout Studio

This book is dedicated to the Lord Jesus Christ,
the only perfect man the world has ever known.

Contents

Introduction	xiii
Chapter 1: Nobody Cares About Last Year	1
Chapter 2: You Can't Worry About That	11
Chapter 3: Don't Be Stupid	21
Chapter 4: My Way or the Highway	31
Chapter 5: Get Out of the Stands	43
Chapter 6: No Excuses	53
Chapter 7: Confidence vs. Arrogance	61
Chapter 8: Be Perfect	71
Chapter 9: Fear	85
Chapter 10: Can You Go?	101
Chapter 11: Know Where You Are Going	113
Chapter 12: What Is a Man?	123
Chapter 13: A True Original	137
Epilogue	149
Chapter Questions	157
Acknowledgments	171
About the Author	175

Introduction

I don't remember the first time I noticed it, but I can see the image in my mind: my dad methodically walking in the rain as if nothing were happening. He is determined. He isn't picking up his pace. He isn't distracted. He isn't covering his head. He is walking as if no rain is falling on him at all.

William "Bill" Burgess was born on January 26, 1941 in Birmingham, Alabama. Like many babies born in the 40s, Dad was born at home and weighed around nine pounds. Even as a child, he was as thick and strong as the steel that made his hometown famous. He was the first son of William Calvin Burgess (whose friends called him "Shorty" even though he was over six feet tall) and Margaret Burgess. Shorty was blue-collar to the core, working the coal mines and the steel mills and eventually retiring from the pipe shop. He was a laid-back man who was often mistaken for the actor James Garner.

My grandparents were quite the pair. Shorty was one of twelve brothers and sisters who were all characters in their own rights. He loved to fish as much as any man alive and was a committed practical joker. Then there was Margaret Burgess, who, to put it mildly, was much more intense. She was the ultimate matriarch. She was very serious, loved Jesus, and was constantly present at her local church. There wasn't a committee that did not feature Margaret Burgess, including the choir. My grandparents had an indelible hand in who my dad would become.

My dad was always around a football field. He played football at Jones Valley High School in Birmingham, graduating in 1958. He was a standout high school player, according to not only his family, who told tall tales of his prowess (including the story of Dad breaking another player's helmet) while playing both ways at fullback and linebacker but also to those he faced. A gentleman once told me that he faced Dad in high school and could still remember the intensity of my dad's eyes looking up at him from the fullback position, ready to destroy anyone who dared to stand in his path.

The stories must have had a kernel of truth because Dad would eventually draw the attention of college coaches such as the University of Alabama's legendary coach, Paul "Bear" Bryant, and Auburn University's revered coach, Ralph "Shug" Jordan. Dad chose to play his college football at Auburn, mainly because he loved the outdoors and the draw of a smaller, more rural college suited him. He would play fullback and linebacker for the Tigers from 1958 to 1963.

In August of 1963, my dad married his high school sweetheart and the love of his life, Geynell White. Mom and Dad honeymooned in beautiful Montgomery, Alabama for the weekend before Dad reported to his first-ever coaching job as an assistant to George "Shorty" White at Banks High School in Birmingham the following Monday. (Unlike my grandfather, George White was called "Shorty" because he was actually short.

Only in Alabama could two men have the same nickname for two completely different reasons.)

Dad would not be an assistant long. Banks High School's chief rival, Woodlawn High, came calling to make Dad their head coach at the ripe age of twenty-five. He would coach Woodlawn High School from 1966 to 1970. But in 1970, the Superintendent of Oxford High School in Oxford, Alabama, asked Shorty White who Alabama's best young football coach was. Coach White quickly replied, "Bill Burgess." Oxford High School offered my dad the head coach and athletic director job, and Dad gathered up his wife and two little boys and headed east to raise his family in Oxford. (Dad and Mom would add a daughter during their time in Oxford, rounding out the young family.)

Dad coached at Oxford High from 1971 to 1985 until Jacksonville State University offered him the head coach position, which he accepted. He would go on to coach the JSU Gamecocks from 1985 to 1997, reaching the postseason multiple times and winning Jacksonville's only national championship in 1992.

Bill Burgess has been inducted into the Division II College Football Hall of Fame, the Gulf South Conference Hall of Fame, the Alabama Sports Hall of Fame, the Jacksonville State Hall of Fame, the Alabama Sports Hall of Fame, and the Alabama High School Hall of Fame. He coached various conference championships both in college and high school. Over the years, I have only ever met two types of people: those influenced by Bill Burgess and those who never met him.

From my first memory of him to the day he died, my dad was a man of steel. Six feet of nothing but hard-nosed strength. My siblings and I were the only people that could say, "My dad can beat up your dad," and it would almost be universally true. Dad coached football for thirty-five years at both the high school and college level. Dad was old school all the way. I have said this many times, but if my dad were coaching today, he would be in jail!

When you played for Coach Bill Burgess, you followed a set of expectations that might as well have been set in stone. You had a sensible haircut. You wore your helmet the entire game, whether on the field or on the sidelines. There were no piercings. You tucked your jersey into your pants and came onto the field in a straight line. There was no dancing in the end zone, and you must play physical football on the field. These rules, and others like them, set the tone for life on and off the field.

It wasn't just the rules that made my dad the man he was. His appearance was straight out of central casting. What did Dad look like? Picture a football field in the heart of Alabama on a hot August day. The temperature is about ninety-nine degrees with what feels like 100% humidity. There, in the middle of the field, stands a coach. On his head is a ballcap with the team logo on the front. (Please never suggest he wear a visor.) He is wearing a collared coach's shirt with the team logo embroidered on the left breast. (You will never see him in a suit and tie, a sweatshirt, or a T-shirt, and please never ever suggest a pullover.) He does not wear sweatpants but instead is perpetually decked out in the unforgettable (and unforgettably tight) coach's shorts. No matter the temperature, even on those rare occasions, maybe twice a season, when the Alabama temperature would dip to the low forties, the shorts remained. The brand of the shorts was "Bike," and my dad may have been the sole reason they were in business. He is clad in black coach's shoes and has white tube socks pulled up over his legendary massive calves. He will wear the same pair until the elastic inevitably gives out and they fall around his ankles.

Dad's calves were the topic of many conversations. Players would marvel and ask, "How did Coach get such massive calves?" Were they merely genetic, or were they earned? Were they a product of the thousands of stadium steps he ran and made his teams run over the years? Were they a result of the many years of playing fullback and linebacker? The calves took on their own legendary status. Stories were told, including one where a snake bit Dad in the calf, only to be unable to penetrate the skin. One version of the story had the snake's teeth breaking.

The outfit was finished off with the ultimate coaching accessory: the coach's whistle. Dad would wear it on a string around his neck. The tip of the whistle would have a couple of bands of white athletic tape stained with tobacco juice. If there was one thing Dad was sure of, it was that white athletic tape could solve any problem. He carried a roll with him at all times. There wasn't an injury or equipment malfunction that athletic tape couldn't fix.

That is the picture of my dad doing what he did best: coaching.

My dad was old school in every way, especially his overall coaching philosophy. Dad loved defense. He truly believed that the best athletes should play defense and that each should be one of the eleven meanest people on the team. He believed that the offense should never consider running anything other than the triple option; to suggest otherwise was to show your stupidity. (If you didn't like the triple option, you were likely one of those who thought the forward pass was a good idea.) Dad was a gifted leader and the type of man admired by other men. He was the type of man other men followed.

I don't recall Bill Burgess being afraid of anyone or anything. He always thought he could take anyone. One of my favorite stories about my dad happened when I called him on his seventy-seventh birthday. It went about like this:

ME: Hey, Pop! Happy Birthday!

DAD: Which one is this?

ME: It's Rick, Dad. I wanted to call and wish you a happy birthday—seventy-seven years old!

DAD: Is Muhammad Ali still alive?

ME: What?

DAD: Is Muhammad Ali still alive?

ME: No, Dad. Muhammad Ali passed away a couple of years ago.

DAD: OK, then, that settles it. There ain't a seventy-seven-year-old man alive who can whip me!

And there you have it. That's Bill Burgess in a nutshell. He played college football as linebacker/fullback at Auburn University for the legendary coach Ralph "Shug" Jordan. People still send me his SEC trading card from the 1950s. My favorite part is the back. Where other cards listed the player's stats, the only thing on the back of Dad's card is the phrase, "He loved contact." That is all you need to know about the intensity he brought to every day of his life. The only opponent that ever managed to slow him down was Alzheimer's. It proved to be his toughest challenge.

My dad taught me so much. To many, he was "Coach." But to my siblings and me, he was "Dad." I loved him dearly and am thankful for his influence on me. He gave me the gift of a work ethic. He taught me how to protect and love my wife by modeling a single-minded devotion to my mother. He taught me not to try to live vicariously through my children, as so many men are prone to do, and to let them find their own dreams and aspirations. He taught me to tell stories and enjoy a loud, hardy laugh. He gave me an appreciation for the outdoors and what a gift from God it was to just be in the woods, listening to the sounds of creation. He taught me that the people who think I am awful and those who think I am great are both wrong. Dad would tell me not to listen to either group. He said you are somewhere in the middle of the two opinions.

Dad won championships. But when Jacksonville State University decided to move up a division, the legendary coach with the ballcap and Bike shorts would eventually be patted on the back, thanked for the contribution, and let go. Like he always did, Dad once again kept everything in perspective. Years later, I remember we were back on the field, this time as a family, when the school was naming the field after him. This was a huge honor, even though Dad always believed that head coaches usually got too much credit and too much blame. Dad was all about the proper balance.

Our family was on the field together as Dad received this wonderful honor. In front of a packed stadium, the announcer had begun the presentation. I was standing next to Dad, and as the announcer was drawing everyone's attention to the field, Dad leaned over to me and said, "Remember, Son, the people who will one day want to name the field after you are the same ones who fired you." And then he smiled at me and looked forward. Classic Bill Burgess.

He was like no other man I have ever known. Everywhere I go, I run into men who tell me Dad was the most influential man in their lives. His legacy lives on in the lives of so many men, but this book is about how he impacted *my* life. Far too many men have fathers who either weren't there at all or were passive or apathetic. I encounter men all the time in the course of my ministry whose fathers were either destructive forces or were completely absent. While I can imagine what their lives must have been like, I cannot relate. My father shaped my life and my faith.

This book is my attempt to share my father's lessons with the world, as a testimony to him and as a way of passing along his lessons to others. Along the way, I will weave in where I see Dad's character and his lessons rooted in the Bible. That is what made his lessons lasting. They were built on the sound principles of God's Word. That is what makes them timeless.

I have much to say, and I appreciate you joining me on this journey. But before we move on, let's return to my dad, walking through a parking lot in the rain. I am not sure how old I would have been, but my guess is that I was around thirteen years old. I found myself alongside my dad, keeping up with him as we walked through a downpour. Wanting to get out of the rain, I started to run for the truck until my dad's massive forearm stopped me dead in my tracks.

I looked up at the rain dripping off the bill of his ever-present cap, which featured the logo of the team he was coaching at the time. I looked into those eyes that never showed even a speck of fear and heard these words: "Son, men don't run in the rain." And there it was—another timeless lesson in a life full of them.

On page 157, you will find a list of optional application questions that allow an individual or a small group to process the truths covered in the chapters. To get more out of the spiritual concepts discussed in each chapter, turn to page 158 and work through the questions to consider how to apply the truths to your life.

Chapter 1
Nobody Cares About Last Year

My dad never cared much for accolades that were heaped upon rookie players. I was never fortunate enough to play for my dad in college, but I played for him for three years in high school. Dad ran an excellent program at Oxford High School in Oxford, Alabama. It was rare that a season did not include his team playing for a regional championship. Due to this success, his high school varsity teams almost always featured only junior and senior players. There was almost never a sophomore on the sidelines, much less in the starting lineup. The sophomore players were usually regulated to the junior varsity team, or, as we call it, the "B Team."

This is why it was noteworthy that in the fall of 1980, our high school team was coming off a subpar season; it just didn't happen. The senior class was small and had not been very successful. They were a very scrappy bunch with a few outstanding players, but it was the class that followed them that most believed would give Oxford High School its first state championship.

I was a sophomore in 1980, when, surprisingly, four of my teammates and I were pulled up to the varsity team. This was highly irregular, but the coaching staff had decided that the five of us were needed to provide some depth. You cannot imagine five guys more pumped up, in no small part because we would each get to wear the coveted Oxford High School gold uniform pants.

The official school colors for Oxford High School are black and gold. The gold isn't yellow but more of an "old gold." If you played football at Oxford High School in the Bill Burgess era, you never were allowed to wear the old gold pants until you made it to Varsity. If you played from the seventh grade through your B Team year, you would have only ever worn white practice pants in the games. We all dreamed of the day we got to walk out of the locker room wearing those old gold football pants. In a highly unusual turn of events, five sophomores would be honored to wear them.

Things went better for me and my friends than we could have imagined. When fall practices ended leading up to that season, not only did we stick with the team, but I was one of four sophomores in the starting lineup. The fifth would also get plenty of playing time by the season's end. The 1980 Oxford Yellow Jackets ended up having a good season. We would win the region championship and move on to the state playoffs, where we would lose to one of the top teams in our classification by one point on the game's last play. Though we fell short of the ultimate goal, it was a very successful year.

Heading into the fall of 1981, we all arrived confident that we had a team with enough talent and depth to win it all. I remember how much different this fall practice felt compared to the previous year. I wasn't nervous at all. I was very confident. My fellow sophomores, now juniors, and I had played really well, and there was a ton of excitement surrounding our junior season. Many opposing coaches and sportswriters thought we had played well enough to warrant some awards. But Bill Burgess didn't put juniors up for awards.

My dad firmly believed that accolades received too early in a player's career impacted their development. Players who received too much praise too soon usually failed to live up to their potential. Many of them had a tendency to coast, living off the success of the past rather than buckling down and continuing to strive for excellence. My dad had seen too many young players begin to think they had arrived. They lost humility.

Proverbs 27:2 says, "Let another praise you, and not your own mouth; a stranger and not your own lips." My dad was a man of many sayings. He had a special one for those who tooted their own horn, especially if they did so prematurely. Dad would listen to a person going on about their performance or about their achievements and say, "You know the thing about an empty wagon? It rattles really, really loudly." Dad didn't put it quite like Solomon in Proverbs, but the point is still the same.

In the fall of 1981, I wasn't quite rattling like an empty wagon, but I can look back and admit that I wasn't overly concerned about my spot in the starting lineup. As far as I was concerned, it was a done deal.

It was August, and in Alabama, that means blazing hot weather. I have often said that practicing twice daily in the Alabama August heat may have delayed my redemption because I wasn't afraid of Hell. A preacher would talk about how hot it was in Hell, and I would lean over to my brother and whisper, "I wonder if it's humid?"

It was the first day of full pads, and we were transitioning into the team portion of practice, which simply means that the full offense goes against the full defense for a period of time. I played defensive tackle, and after the first play of the full pads practice, I heard the whistle blow. As the play stopped, I noticed my dad approaching the defense with a look that never meant anything good. I can still see the sweat glistening off that face that looked like it was chiseled out of pure granite, the face that would strike fear in anyone who opposed this mountain of a man. His massive calves bulged as he picked up momentum, and he headed for the defense. It was apparent he wasn't thrilled with something, and it didn't take long for me to realize that something was me.

My dad's voice was in a class by itself. His mother, whom we called MeMaw, said that Dad had a beautiful baritone voice. Of course, she was never on one of his football teams or set fire to the woods behind the house when she was ten years old. Had she done either, she might understand that "beautiful" didn't apply to that voice.

Dad's voice required no bullhorn as it pierced Alabama's thick, humid air and was likely heard by anyone within a mile of the practice field. That voice directed its full force at me and ordered me to stand on the sideline. I was replaced by another player, one my dad said actually wanted to earn a spot on the team and wasn't as likely to loaf on the next play as I had just done.

Looking back on this interaction forty-plus years later, I don't think I loafed at all. That has never been my style. I am pretty sure my dad didn't believe I had, either. But Dad was a great leader and motivator. He was a master at this process. He knew what harm a little success could cause such a young player.

As I sat there watching my replacement take the reps at the position I had understood to be mine, my dad walked over and stood beside me. I will never forget what he said in a voice only I could hear: "Son, nobody cares what you did last year." And there it was: the lesson.

My dad was trying to tell me that last year's accolades didn't earn me a starting position on this year's team. He taught me early on not to rest on your laurels. Was I going to live off the stellar sophomore season I had? Or would I show everyone what an even better junior year I would have? Last year's performance isn't good enough for this year. You are either getting better or getting worse. It's impossible to be the same.

Men, what a profound truth this is for our spiritual lives. Too many men live on last year's (or last decade's) spiritual growth. We must ask ourselves, "Are we growing in our relationship with Christ, or are we fading?" What efforts are we making to ensure that we are growing and getting stronger in our faith?

There's a very interesting story in Acts 8. It's the story of Philip and the Ethiopian eunuch. You remember Philip, who would come to be known as Philip the Evangelist in church history, was one of the seven deacons chosen by the apostles in the early church to help distribute food to widows and serve the community (Acts 6:1–6). Philip was known for his strong faith and was described as full of the Holy Spirit. Philip quickly became known not only for his service but also for his powerful preaching and evangelism. In other words, he was the kind of guy you want on your team, a faithful jack of all spiritual trades.

In Acts 8, Philip is directed by an angel of the Lord to go south on the road from Jerusalem to Gaza. This was somewhat of an unexpected request because this was a desert road, more or less in the middle of nowhere. On the way, Philip meets an Ethiopian eunuch, an important official in charge of the treasury for the queen of the Ethiopians, who is returning from worshiping in Jerusalem. The Ethiopian is reading aloud from the book of Isaiah, which must have gotten Philip's radar up. He had to sense that this was why the Spirit had led him there.

The Spirit prompted Philip to approach the chariot. Philip addressed the Ethiopian, at which point the eunuch admitted that he did not understand what he was reading. The Ethiopian invited Philip to sit with him, and Philip explained the passage, showing how it pointed to Jesus. He shared the good news of the Gospel with him.

As they traveled, they encountered some water, and the Ethiopian asked to be baptized. Philip baptized him. If the story stopped there, it would be miraculous enough. But here's where it gets wild. We're told in Acts 8:39–40 that when the Ethiopian came up out of the water, "the Spirit of the Lord carried Philip away, and the eunuch saw him no more, and went on his way rejoicing."

But Philip found himself at Azotus, and as he passed through, he "preached the Gospel to all the towns until he came to Caesarea." Every part of this story is absolutely amazing. Can you imagine how Philip must have felt? Being led by the Spirit, experiencing this fruitful, meaningful encounter, and then being whisked away by the Spirit to a different city entirely? It's so much it's hard to even fathom.

Men, let's be honest with ourselves. If we were in Philip's shoes, many of us would have lived off the eunuch story for years. We would have got so much mileage out of it. We would have told it repeatedly, wringing every bit of glory out of it. Many men would have had this experience and rested on the laurels of that great moment of being used by God. Aren't we glad Phillip didn't do that? Scripture and church history tell us that Philip later settled in Caesarea, where he is described as having four daughters who also prophesied (Acts 21:8–9). His legacy is that of an obedient, Spirit-led evangelist who played a crucial role in spreading the Gospel beyond Jewish communities, demonstrating God's heart for all nations. It never crossed his mind to live on last season's growth.

I encounter too many men who still rattle on about that one mission trip they took twenty years ago and haven't done much for the Kingdom since. There's nothing wrong with remembering our past spiritual victories. But if there aren't fresh ones to celebrate, what are we doing? This isn't the example we see from the early church leaders. When it came to their obedience and faithfulness, they were never satisfied that they had done enough. They seized every opportunity to reach one more person for Christ or preach the Gospel. They didn't see themselves as having arrived. They were constantly pushing for more.

It's amazing that Jesus gave up His very life on the cross to purchase our lives. Yet, the response of many Christian men is to live off their past spiritual experiences. That's not the life Jesus bought for us.

When did you last pour yourself out for the Kingdom of God? Was it this year? I hope so because nobody cares what you did last year.

Chapter 2
You Can't Worry About That

My dad was the toughest man I have ever known, and it's not even close. I can't think of anyone I've ever known who even approaches the level of toughness of Bill Burgess. Dad's toughness manifested itself in a variety of ways over the years. But one of the main ways, and a way that definitely impacted those around him, was the fact that my dad never believed anyone was truly sick or injured. Not really. He was so tough that he sincerely believed a person could simply refuse to be sick. He believed one *might* be hurting, but they weren't truly injured. To believe otherwise was to be soft. To Bill Burgess, it was all just a matter of willpower.

These traits were on full display one hot, humid day in Alabama during an afternoon practice amid "two-a-days." I don't know how many of you reading this have ever been to Alabama in August before, but to say it's hot and humid is an understatement. It is very, very hot and very, very humid. Imagine temperatures in the upper nineties to low one hundreds. The average August humidity is in the 70–80% range, which drives the heat index well above one hundred degrees most days. And we played football in this weather. Twice each day. Don't miss that these were full-contact practices, both in the morning and the afternoon practices. This was a special kind of misery.

On this particular day, as the story goes, my dad was coaching Oxford High School. He addressed the team before the second practice of the day and made sure that everyone understood what was ahead. He wanted everyone's expectations to be the same, specifically regarding how tough it was going to be. He launched into an epic speech that, before it was over, would become a legendary moment that would be talked about for years to come.

Dad began to tell the team that they were going to be hot. The temperature was already sweltering. Then he would say, "You can't worry about that." Dad made the point that we all decided to play football in August in Alabama.

He then went on to say that they were going to be tired. After all, we were well into two-a-days. It was exhausting on every level. We were being driven about as hard as you could drive teenagers. But Dad had a solution for our fatigue: "You can't worry about that." Of course, we were tired. We'd been colliding with each other for hour after hour each day.

Finally, Dad said that many of our bodies were aching and sore. Again, Dad passed along the secret to dealing with the pain: "You can't worry about that. This is a contact sport," Dad said. "You hit, and you get hit. You can't worry about that." Are you starting to pick up the speech's theme yet? In my dad's world, nothing could keep you from rising to the occasion if you simply decided in your mind to press on and stop thinking about the obstacle. He embodied "mind over matter" more than anyone I have ever met. But what happened next changed the lives of the people who witnessed it.

Various former players have told and retold what happened at the end of my dad's speech that day over the years. It has taken a life all of its own, and for good reason. It was as shocking as it was inspiring, and it personified everything about my dad's approach to discomfort and pain.

Picture him: standing in the Alabama sun giving this speech, surrounded by a semi-circle of players on a knee, coaching cap perched on his head, black coaching shoes, tube socks that had no elastic because the massive calves were more than the elastic could handle, coaching shirt with the embroidered team logo half tucked into those ever-present coach's shorts, so tight that no gender confusion was possible. Can you see him there, like a statue baking in the Alabama summer sun? He was the vision of old-school football authority. But as he was wrapping up his speech, the afternoon's silence was disturbed by an unexpected sound.

Suddenly, a voice from the second row pointed out something that no one else had noticed, or maybe they had noticed but simply didn't have the courage to speak. The player's name has been forever lost in the passage of time. As the years have rolled by, some claim they know who said it, but to my knowledge, no one has ever stepped forward to accept responsibility. This anonymous voice piped up and timidly announced, "Hey, Coach, did you know you are standing in an ant colony?" What happened next has impacted those players who witnessed it for the rest of their lives.

It took my dad a moment to register that someone else was speaking. Everyone I have ever talked to since, who was there that day and witnessed that event, agrees that my dad responded by squinting his eyes in disgust, slowly looking down at his fire ant-covered calves, and then raising his head to fix his steady gaze back on the team. Without moving a muscle, my dad scanned the team before him and uttered what is now a famous line, "See, this is exactly what I am talking about. You can't worry about that."

You can't worry about that. Are there fire ants covering your lower limbs? You can't worry about that. Are they biting your legs? You can't worry about that. Mind over matter. Nothing to see here.

Some say that the ants gave up trying to bite those massive calves and began to crawl off his body in fear, ashamed at their incursion, humbled to return back to where they came. I remember Dad simply taking a step forward and ordering the team to start practice. I will never forget that moment as long as I live.

Dad's message was clear: we cannot dwell on or be anxious about the difficulty of the journey. As we strive to accomplish our goal, we must focus not on the hardships but on the finish line. When imagining the payoff, the pain and discomfort of the moment fade away.

Scripture speaks to followers of Christ in much the same way. In James 5:11, James tells us to be patient in suffering. In

James 1:2–4, he instructs us to count it all joy when we suffer due to the benefits it creates. In 1 Peter 1:6–7, Peter tells us to rejoice in difficulty because we should understand that this has been deemed necessary to test the genuineness of our faith. Jesus said that we should take heart when we experience trials because He has already won victory over the world (John 16:33). And many other places throughout the Bible speak to this same concept. However, I want to focus on a point that the Apostle Paul makes in the book of 2 Corinthians.

The Apostle Paul planted churches throughout the Roman Empire. Some of these churches were healthier than others. Take the Corinthian church, for example. The church had ongoing problems that Paul addressed in his letters to them. Paul actually had enemies within the church, and as a result, he was forced to defend his integrity as an apostle for Christ.

As a part of this, in 2 Corinthians 11, Paul discusses the difficulties he had faced due to his devotion to Christ. It is a list worth reading here, especially considering what we have just been discussing. In describing the hardships he had faced in service of the Lord, Paul said:

> "Are they servants of Christ? I am a better one—I am talking like a madman—with far greater labors, far more imprisonments, with countless beatings, and often near death. Five times I received at the hands of the Jews the forty lashes less one. Three times I was beaten with rods. Once I was stoned. Three times I was shipwrecked; a night and a day I was adrift at sea; on frequent journeys, in danger from rivers, danger from robbers, danger from my own people, danger from Gentiles,

danger in the city, danger in the wilderness, danger at sea, danger from false brothers; in toil and hardship, through many a sleepless night, in hunger and thirst, often without food, in cold and exposure. And, apart from other things, there is the daily pressure on me of my anxiety for all the churches." (2 Corinthians 11:23–28)

As you read Paul's resume of suffering, don't miss in verse 24 that Paul noted five times that he was beaten with "forty lashes less one." There is so much in this list of trials and hardships Paul endured, but for our conversation, I want to focus on this particular punishment administered by those who opposed Paul's devotion to Christ.

The "forty lashes less one" is a kind of corporal punishment outlined in Deuteronomy 25:1–3. The Law allowed for lashings as punishment but limited it to 40 lashes to ensure those administering the punishment didn't get carried away. God was ensuring His people practiced restraint so they didn't humiliate their brothers or sisters or permanently injure the person receiving the punishment. By Paul's time, however, Jewish leaders only gave thirty-nine lashes (forty "less one"). Remember, these Pharisees were hyper-focused on keeping the rules of the Law (even though they routinely violated the spirit of the Law). They did thirty-nine to keep from accidentally miscounting and going over.

This was a brutal punishment. The lashes were given using a whip made of leather strips, which, as we can imagine, would be quite painful. There would be scars. It was common for the lashes to be divided, with two-thirds on the back of the body and one-third on the front. And Paul said he experienced this five times!

Here's something important for us to understand. I want this to be clear as we consider everything Paul went through: thirty-nine lashes were the max, but not the required number. Don't miss that. If the Jews were beating someone for a punishment and the person's spirit was broken at twenty lashes, they could and would stop. Maybe for some people, they broke after five lashes. Maybe others, it was ten. But not Paul. On five separate occasions, Paul took the "forty less one."

Do you see the point? They beat Paul five times, giving him the maximum amount of lashes every single time. By their own laws, they could not beat him anymore. How incredible that no matter how much they threw at Paul, they could never get him to break! Paul was a thirty-nine-lash man. How about you?

When we consider the trials we go through in our service of Christ, it's important to consider whether we are thirty-nine-lash men. Or does any difficulty cause us to shrink back and reject Christ in the public arena? Do you run at the first sign of inconvenience or hardship? Do you give up when standing up for the Gospel becomes difficult?

I remember being honored to speak alongside Becket Cook at a Promise Keepers event in New York City, NY. Becket Cook was raised by followers of Christ only to reject the faith and live his life as a homosexual man for many years as a successful set designer in Hollywood. (You can read his entire story in the book *Change of Affection*.) I will never forget when he began to tell the story of what his conversion to Christ as an adult cost him. It cost him his job, his friends, his standing in Hollywood, the trendy parties, and so on. But his response to "losing these things" stuck with me. Becket said, "Look at all I have gained! I have gained Christ. I have gained redemption! I have gained eternal life!" What a powerful testimony.

Paul would have agreed with Becket Cook. As they beat him, we know he focused on the goal, not his circumstances. We know because he told us so:

> "But whatever gain I had, I counted as loss for the sake of Christ. Indeed, I count everything as loss because of the surpassing worth of knowing Christ Jesus my Lord. For his sake I have suffered the loss of all things and count them as rubbish, in order that I may gain Christ and be found in him, not having a righteousness of my own that comes from the law, but that which comes through faith in Christ, the righteousness from God that depends on faith—that I may know him and the power of his resurrection, and may share his sufferings, becoming like him in his death, that by any means possible I may attain the resurrection from the dead." (Philippians 3:7–11)

Paul considered all that he lost for the sake of Christ, all the pain and punishment, nothing but garbage compared to gaining Christ. He knew the cost. He measured it. And he decided that to be in the service of our King was worth more than anything this world had to offer.

There can be no doubt. Our devotion to Christ will cost us. But in the words of Bill Burgess, "We can't worry about that."

Chapter 3
Don't Be Stupid

My entire life, it seemed like my dad was on a mission to eradicate stupidity from the world. He had a deep disdain for it. The problem is that this passion of his regularly conflicted with my tendency to do stupid things. This often put me in the position to hear some of his most colorful analogies concerning the topic.

When I played for Dad in high school, I discovered that I apparently did things that caused him to marvel at my stupidity. Dad had some sayings about stupidity that bordered on the bizarre. And the seasons I played for him, I heard many of them, some so wild that I would ask myself where in the world he came up with this stuff. I can't recall exactly what I did that summoned one of Dad's most classic beauties, but I will never forget the words that flowed from his mouth.

I can still see him standing there in the middle of the practice field. Something I did caused him to stare at me with those frustrated eyes, squinting with disgust. I could see his mind turning, working to capture exactly how he felt about my blunder. Today, all these decades later, I can still hear the detailed description of my stupidity that rolled out of his mouth: "Rick, what you just did was so stupid that if they put your brain in a hummingbird, it would fly backward up a mule's butt." (The original, slightly more colorful word he used instead of "butt" has been altered.)

I couldn't believe what I heard. What sort of brilliant mind comes up with this analogy? In the years since, I have spent much time considering his handiwork. Breaking it down into its parts allows one to survey its majesty. Let's start with the hummingbird. I guess I understand the application here: a person (me) with a brain so small that it would fit in a hummingbird would be stupid. OK, got it. Most people would stop here. Dad had made his point. But no, this man needed to paint a much clearer picture.

The hummingbird in the analogy is now confused. Why? It has my brain in it. And apparently, my brain lacks so much intelligence that the tiny bird can no longer fly forward. It's now flying backward. That's how much distress my gaffe had caused my dad.

However, this master of the metaphor wasn't done. He took it to the next and final level to drive home the point. He introduced the actual destination for the backward-flying tiny bird with the tiny brain.

The destination he chose for the hummingbird was a mule's butt. What an artist! How many other men knew how to paint such a clear picture of stupidity, one that no one would ever forget? And it's not like this was Dad's only colorful phrase in his one-man crusade to stamp out stupidity. Dad had so many of these that he would drop at any moment. Want another beauty?

If you'd like another one of Dad's big hits, there's a good story that precedes it.

I am not sure of our age, but my brother and I were playing in the wooded area behind our home with our friends. We loved being in those woods. We built forts, caught various creatures and tried to make them pets, fought imaginary battles, and shot things with our Daisy BB guns. That day, we broke a rule most children know you simply don't break. We decided we would play with matches.

"Do not play with matches" is a foundational rule every parent tells every child that has ever been born. And yet, on this day, we chose to ignore that rule. I remember that it had been very dry that season, so our brilliant idea to light small dried pine limbs that had fallen to the ground and stomp them out before they could do any real damage was doomed to fail.

In our minds, these pine branches were the torches we had seen explorers on TV light to explore caves and other exciting places. As kids will do, one of our friends let his torch burn a little longer and panicked when the flames got close to his hand. To avoid being burned, he tossed the torch into *very* dry weeds, which ignited a brush fire. At that moment, I remember suddenly realizing something: Smokey Bear was the least of our worries. A much bigger bear was to be feared, namely our dad!

The wooded area we played in was more than an acre from our home. We were children of the 1970s when the houses were small, but the yards were huge. I began to run across that huge yard to the hose pipe and the ever-present plastic bucket (that stayed full for the yard dogs to get a drink if needed). I was filling the bucket with water when my dad rounded the corner of the house. I will never forget what he looked like. He was speaking at a banquet that night, and he wore a green leisure suit nearly as tight as the one I had seen Tom Jones wear on *The Tonight Show*. It was a far cry from the daily wardrobe of coaching shorts and trucker hats.

Dad stopped in his tracks and looked down at me. He asked why I was filling up a bucket with water. Looking back, I cannot believe how calmly I answered this question. It just came out: "For the fire." Just like that, straightforward and matter-of-fact. Dad looked at me with a look I would come to recognize on multiple occasions throughout my life. His eyes narrowed as he looked out over the yard, just past the dog pen, and saw the smoke from the fire. Dad grabbed the bucket and started up the yard in his green leisure suit and dress shoes.

At this moment, I began to consider making a run for it. I remember thinking I could make it to Taylor's Grocery before he returned from putting out the fire. Maybe I could work for Mrs. Taylor, maybe start a new life stocking shelves and cleaning up. Surely, she'd have mercy on me and let me live at her grocery store. But I didn't run to Taylor's. I started following Dad. My curiosity got the best of me. I had to see what was going to happen.

As an adult, I know this isn't true, but as a child, it seemed that it was actually the fire that was afraid of my dad and not the other way around. Dad poured the water on some of the flames, and that helped, but then he began to stomp the fire with his dress shoes. He repeated this until the fire was no more, and only the smoke remained. Crisis averted.

I can't imagine what someone watching would have said about that day. When Dad walked out of that smoke, he had every kid, including my little brother, in his hands. It was a different time back then; Dad deservedly scolded every one of us, and not one parent got upset about his actions. The only calls my parents got from the other boys' parents were calls of gratitude and a promise to discipline us if we ever did anything out of line in their presence. Dad sent everyone home, and then it was just the three of us. Dad, my brother, and me. This was the moment of truth.

Dad stared at us, eyes squinting in his trademark look of exasperation, and then abruptly walked inside. There was still a banquet to go to. He had to change out of the smokey leisure suit and shoes before he and Mom left for the banquet. Our babysitter had arrived. Mom walked out looking beautiful but rightfully concerned for our well-being. She was thankful, I'm sure, that she would at least still have my sister around after Dad was done with us.

It appeared the banquet had saved us, at least for the moment. As Dad and Mom walked out, they told us to sit on the couch and not move until they returned. Dad was just about to turn and leave when he stopped, looked at my brother and me sitting there on that couch, and dropped what became a classic Bill Burgess line: "I tell you what, boys. If I had ordered a truckload of stupid people and all I got were you two, I would have gotten my money's worth." Then he turned and walked out the door. There were no TV remotes in those days, but we did not dare leave that couch to change the channel, just in case Dad was to walk in and find us disobeying his instructions. Plus, the TV show *Hee Haw* was on.

Did you know that the Bible actually addresses the stupidity of humankind? It defines what it means to be stupid. It's right there in Proverbs. Did you know that the Bible actually says that those who hate reproof are stupid? Proverbs 12:1 says, "Whoever loves discipline loves knowledge, but he who hates reproof is stupid." That's right. The wise man is the one who *desires* discipline. The man the Bible says is knowledgeable (the opposite of stupid) is the one who wants to experience the growth that comes with discipline, which is the opposite of how we typically think of discipline.

We don't often think about discipline as a positive thing, but when it's the Lord doing the discipline, it is always positive. Why? Because God's discipline is Him bringing us in line with His character and His expectation of what His people should be like. And so the wise man wants discipline. It's how David could say in Psalm 119:34–35, "Give me understanding, that I may keep your law and observe it with my whole heart. Lead me in the path of your commandments, for I delight in it." David is begging to know God's rules so he can follow them. He tells God that he "delights" in God's rules. Men, can we say the same? Are you someone who loves the rules of God and wants God to do whatever it takes to keep you in line with them? That's a man who loves wisdom and hates stupidity.

The Bible goes on to say that people who are what I call "sin daredevils" are stupid.

Proverbs 14:16 says, "One who is wise is cautious and turns away from evil, but a fool is reckless and careless." Solomon is saying here that it's wise to stay away from things that will lead us to sin. Too many of us play games with sin. We see how close we can get to sin without actually committing sin. Or we flippantly commit what we consider "small" sins, keeping away from the "big" ones, when Scripture clearly shows that all sin corrupts. All sin leads us down the path toward moral stupidity. When we play daredevil with sin, we're the opposite of wise. This leads to nothing but trouble.

Solomon has more to say about the stupid man. He says in Proverbs 14:17 that "a man of quick temper acts foolishly, and a man of evil devices is hated." Do you have a quick temper? Solomon would say you're acting stupidly. Have you ever watched someone lose their temper at the drop of a hat? Does their behavior seem wise to you? Do they look like someone who has the Holy Spirit's guidance and self-control? Of course not. When we can't control our anger, we usually can't control ourselves. The wise man is the man who gets angry and controls it. The stupid man is at the mercy of his emotions.

Finally, Proverbs 28:26 teaches a final valuable lesson. Here, the wisest man ever to live says, "Whoever trusts in his own mind is a fool, but he who walks in wisdom will be delivered." What is God saying to us through Solomon here? God is teaching us that when we don't know what He commands and lean on our own understanding, we are just making it up as we go. We are all flawed, but the wise man understands that deliverance comes through faith in God and living our lives according to His ways.

Are you wise enough to know that apart from a relationship with Jesus, your path will end in destruction, not deliverance? The ultimate form of stupidity is believing that you can work hard enough or follow enough rules to be good enough in God's eyes to get to heaven. The wise man knows that the only real rescue we can hope for is the salvation that comes by surrendering our lives to Jesus and trusting in God's ways, not our own.

The world is full of people who embrace the stupidity of a life apart from God. Let's not be those people. The one and only living God's instruction is perfect. Our flesh isn't. Our sinful nature will never lead us rightly. Let's commit to being wise and not stupid.

Chapter 4
My Way or the Highway

When an individual entered any Bill Burgess-run football program, they figured out pretty quickly that it would be done the Burgess way or it wouldn't be done. This was not a democracy. There was no voting. The system was clear, and the expectations were set in stone. It was Coach Burgess' way, or it was the highway. Either get on board or pack your bags.

I recall talking about this truth to one of his former players soon after my dad left this earth and, as we say in the South, "went on in." The player said something profound that I have thought about often since then. He said that Dad had a way of passing on his personality to everyone in the program. A person might have entered the program thinking and acting a certain way. They may have had a certain outlook on life, a lens through which to view the world around them. But, this former player said, before you knew it, you were becoming just like Coach. You had his expectations of yourself and others. You took on his intensity, not just in football but in all things. I have thought about this comment and wholeheartedly believe it to be true.

Bill Burgess was nothing if not intense. And very few things brought out his intensity as referees did. Now let me be clear: Dad worked referees like a maestro conducting an orchestra. He was vocal from the first whistle (but true to form, players were expected to keep their mouths shut and play the game). I would hear him rumble as he looked at these men dressed like zebras and say loud enough for all to hear, "Here's a man with a part-time job that's gonna cost me a full-time job!"

One of his former college teammates decided to become an official. He thought this might help Dad overcome his disdain for those in stripes or, at the very least, not hold that disdain over him. This man actually said to my dad once that he knew Dad didn't dislike him just because he had chosen to be a referee. Dad replied, "I don't dislike you. Except when you put those stripes on. Then I dislike you." The friend decided to say no more on this subject; I assume he hoped he would never be assigned one of Dad's games.

There are many stories about my dad's interactions with football officials. One time, he disagreed with a call and got flagged for letting his opinion be known a little too vehemently. The opinion might also have included a word or two that his mother would not have tolerated. Dad asked the official why he had dropped the flag when Dad was clearly complaining from the sideline and not on the field of play. The officials responded that the flag was dropped because Dad had used foul language, to which Dad replied, "What are you, a priest?" This got Dad a second flag.

These stories are legendary, and there are many more. However, the one that gets recounted the most occurred in Dad's third season at Jacksonville State University. The first two seasons had not gone well: ten wins, eight losses, and two ties. This was when JSU still played in the Gulf South Conference, and this particular Saturday, they found themselves in a crucial game against Delta State out of Cleveland, Mississippi. The new coaching staff needed to take this team to the playoffs, as the fans and the administration who hired them were starting to wonder whether hiring these high school coaches was a good idea. This was a must-win game.

Dad had already proven his willingness to take risks in order to win. He broke protocol by playing a freshman quarterback, something that didn't happen back then. Dad probably knew he wouldn't catch too much flak for it; this gifted player had a bright future, and the program was in the rebuilding phase. However, conventional wisdom said that Dad should have redshirted the quarterback. (A "redshirt" refers to a player who sits out for a season, thus preserving a year of eligibility without participating in games.)

The discussion about whether to play the young man and lose his redshirt actually broke out on the sideline between Dad and the offensive coordinator earlier in the season. The offense was struggling and needed a boost. Dad called for the freshman phenom to be put into the game. The offensive coordinator told Dad that he might want to reconsider using up the freshman's redshirt year and, instead, plan for the future. Dad turned to the coach and replied, "If you and I don't put him in the game now, we may never see him play." The plan worked, and the new quarterback turned the season around. Now, facing Delta State, a win would put Jacksonville State in a great position to make the playoffs. But a loss would mean that the season was all but over.

As these things often do, it all came down to a fourth and short play for Delta State late in the game. If they got the first down, the drive to win the game would continue. But if JSU stopped them, the game would belong to JSU. If the defense made the stop, then the offense could simply run out the clock. So, on 4th down and short, with every fan in the stadium on their feet, the Jacksonville State Defense rose up and stopped Delta State for no gain. The Delta State fans were crushed. The visiting JSU fans went wild. It certainly appeared to everyone that JSU would win the game. But wait! The only thing that could keep JSU from winning was staring everyone in the face: a flag had been thrown on the play. The game was now in the hands of those very men my dad loathed.

The reason for the flag was this: After the emotion-filled play, a fight broke out on the field. (Dad picked his defensive players by finding the meanest people on the team. At times, that led to "extracurricular activity" on the field that had to be penalized. But as Dad said many times, "I would rather have to tone a player down than have to rev one up.") Of course, someone was going to be penalized for this behavior. The refs conferred, and the call was a personal foul for unsportsmanlike conduct on the Jacksonville State defense!

What a turn of events. For the briefest of moments, everyone thought the tide had turned. Would Delta State get the first down after all and keep their dreams alive? Would Jacksonville

State come this close to victory only to lose it to a penalty? But, after a moment of panic, cooler heads prevailed. The penalty was a "dead-ball foul," meaning it happened after the play ended. The play would stand, JSU would get the ball, and the fifteen-yard penalty would be assessed on JSU's first possession. Crisis averted. JSU would prevail, after all.

What happened next has been the stuff of legend for years. The officials who were there that day and have since moved on to officiate at the highest level still talk about the incident in Cleveland, MS. The official who made the call was a rookie, and either the moment was too big for him, or he simply forgot how to handle a dead-ball foul. So, he begins to mark off the fifteen-yard penalty as if Delta State was retaining possession and getting a new set of downs. Of course, this was incorrect, but it created a moment of extreme chaos. By all accounts, it appeared that Delta State was getting the ball and a first down.

Confusion began to spread across the crowd. You could hear the rumble of conversation as people asked, "Isn't that a dead-ball foul?" Some fans cheered. Some fans booed. The JSU sideline was chaos. The coaches, players, cheerleaders, and band members (the ones who knew the rules) were protesting loudly. How dare this rookie official, this man in zebra stripes, with his part-time job, try to steal the season from the JSU Gamecocks!

We needed a hero, someone to save the day, someone to make this right. But no one who was there could believe what they saw next. Sprinting from the sidelines onto the field of play, fire in his eyes, massive calves bulging, was none other than Coach Bill Burgess. As he ran onto the field, another flag flew in the air, but

Dad's focus was unhindered as he zeroed in on his destination: the game ball!

To everyone's astonishment, Dad did something truly unprecedented. He grabbed the ball and refused to let the rookie referee have it back. He had come so close to winning the game and a trip to the playoffs that he wouldn't let it slip away. The ball would be given to Delta State over his dead body. The small JSU contingency in the stands and the JSU sideline realized their hero had come. They went wild. The Delta State fans, seeing an interloper on the field who had, in essence, stolen the game ball, began to reign down boos. It was absolute chaos as the refs descended on Dad to bring order to a situation that had spiraled out of control. In the center of it all was Bill Burgess, fiercely gripping the game ball. No one had yet pried it from his hands. Who would dare try?

One of the foundational truths at the core of my father's identity was his bedrock belief that no one could take him. No one. According to my dad, no one could block him, no one could tackle him, no one could stop him. One of the most vivid memories of my childhood happened in the backseat of the green Plymouth our parents drove. It perfectly exemplifies Dad's unwavering belief in his physical fortitude.

My little brother, Greg, and I were sitting in the back seat of the Plymouth on the way home from church. That Sunday, we had a guest speaker, a man who played for years in the NFL and then became a professional weightlifter. On the way home, Mom set the table for Dad to talk to his boys about what we should take away from the man's message. Mom said to Dad, "Bill, what did you take away from the speaker's message today?" Even today, I can still see the rearview mirror, looking at Dad's face, waiting for his response. As a young boy, I wondered what Dad took away from this man. I was curious what I was supposed to learn.

Without hesitation, Dad gave his response. Eyes still on the road, straight-faced, he replied, "Well, all I could think about was whether or not this guy thought he could block me." As my mom gasped with exasperation, letting him know in no uncertain terms how she felt about what she deemed an unacceptable answer to her question, my eyes met my dad's in the rearview mirror. They sparkled with mischief, a sly grin breaking across his face. I looked at my brother, and we smiled, agreeing that no one could block our dad.

So it was that we knew not one of these referees could take the ball from Coach, not without his permission. Dad's booming voice carried across the field over the chaos. We could all hear him saying, over and over again, "That's a dead-ball foul! It's our ball." The head official for that game is now over all the NCAA referees. (He loves to tell this story.) He finally was able to calm Dad down. He got my dad to stop carrying on, and when he did, he said the words that everyone had already figured out: "Coach, you are right. That is a dead-ball foul, and I will give your team the ball. But since you have come on the field and taken the ball from us, it will be given to your team a long, long way from here." And, to no one's surprise, Dad was ejected from the game.

Eventually, they did indeed give JSU the ball back, but not after marking off the fifteen yards for the fight after the play, the fifteen yards for Dad's entrance onto the field, and the fifteen additional yards for taking the ball and not letting the officials have it to mark the play. So, Jacksonville State University (finally) had the ball, but instead of losing fifteen yards, we faced "first down and fifty-five." Dad passed the offensive coordinator as he left the field of play to rousing applause. He said, "Hey, we can run out the clock without needing a first down. But if we do need one, don't throw it."

Jacksonville State went on to win the game and went to the playoffs. While this makes for an incredible story, one that is still told in officiating circles, we must acknowledge a simple truth: the head official was almost certainly going to correct the mistake of the rookie ref. It was the wrong call, and the rest of the officiating crew knew it. To avoid thirty yards of penalties and the chaos of the stolen game ball, Dad could have simply stated his case to the head official, who then would have informed the rookie official of his error, and JSU would have been looking at a "first down and twenty-five" with the game in hand. Was Dad correct? One hundred percent. But there was surely a better way to achieve the desired result.

There is a spiritual application here. How often do we try to fix problems our way versus God's way? How often do we try to take things into our own hands without seeing how God will bring about a resolution in His timing? I don't know who was the first to say this, but I recall how impactful it was the first time I heard this quote: "Obedience isn't doing God's will our way or doing our will God's way. True obedience is doing God's will, God's way." That is about as straightforward as it gets. Think about how absurd it is to actually think that our plan for handling things could be better than the perfect plan of the only living God.

Ultimately, it comes down to who we think is in charge, God or us. Do we do things our own way (essentially doing them in our name), or do we do things God's way, in His name? When I think about this concept, I can't help but think about Jesus' words in Matthew 7:21–23: "Not everyone who says to me, 'Lord, Lord,' will enter the kingdom of heaven, but the one who does the will of my Father who is in heaven. On that day many will say to me, 'Lord, Lord, did we not prophesy in your name, and cast out demons in your name, and do many mighty works in your name?' And then will I declare to them, 'I never knew you; depart from me, you workers of lawlessness.'"

These words have been the topic of much debate. What did Jesus mean? Jesus was not talking about true believers who had lost their salvation. No, Jesus was talking about a group of people who claimed to do all sorts of things in the name of Jesus. Jesus, who perfectly knows all people's hearts, says they may be using my name, but He never knew them. They weren't in a relationship. Jesus didn't say that He *once* knew them, but now He doesn't. He says there was never a time when He ever knew them. He doesn't mean their existence was unknown to Him; as God, Jesus is all-knowing. There is no one alive He doesn't have knowledge of. He is saying that there was never a time when these people submitted their lives to Jesus in saving faith, which led to a relationship with God.

Jesus says, in essence, these people are lying about their relationship with God. It may be true that they are *saying* their works were in His name, but the fact is that they weren't. Not really. They may claim to call Jesus "Lord," but they reject His authority in their lives. Instead of being under Jesus' authority, they operate under their own. These people may claim to be doing all this work in Jesus' name, but it's really to glorify their own name.

So why does Jesus say they aren't in a relationship? Why does He say He doesn't "know" them? One must simply look at verse 21b. There it is as plain as day. Jesus says He doesn't know these people because they are not doing the will of His Father. This is why their claim of knowing and serving Jesus is a lie.

These people don't do God's will; they do their will. They have established their own version of obedience, which may bring them glory but doesn't bring glory to God. And they can't claim not to know the will of God now. It's not a matter of ignorance. We know that the will of God is revealed all throughout Scripture. Jesus makes it crystal clear that those who truly love Him are those who truly obey Him, those who say what God says to say, and do what God says to do.

Where do you stand? Do you try to live a "my way or the highway" kind of faith? I hope not. Because regardless of what we think, only one person gets to say that, and it's God.

Chapter 5
Get Out of the Stands

There's nothing better than a good pre-game speech. When the cameras are in the locker rooms, and the coach is captured pumping up his players? It's hard to beat. There have been some epic ones over the years. And the players even get in on it, too. There are legendary stories of players giving fiery half-time speeches to their team and rallying their side for the win. My dad was as good as any at giving speeches. But it was his pre-season speeches that I remember best.

You always looked forward to the pre-season speech if you played on any team my dad coached. This usually happened around the beginning of fall practice, which means August. It was around the first practice, and Dad would gather the team around him for his big speech.

This was when my dad (in a way only he could do) would lay out exactly what players could expect if they wanted to remain on the team. The first thing that was always clearly communicated was that there was no such thing as a democracy or a constitutional republic on Coach Bill Burgess' football field. No sir. No, it was stated, with no uncertainty so that everyone understood, that choosing to stay on the team was entering a dictatorship. And lest there be any doubt, they were looking at the dictator.

Dad would then go on to inform every player that playing time would be earned, not given, regardless of past performance or experience. It didn't matter who you were; each season was a new one. What you did last year didn't matter.

Furthermore, practices were not to be missed for any reason, and you better not let him see your parents walk onto the field during practice. No one was allowed to be late. You had better not show up missing any equipment, and no one was allowed to leave their equipment lying around the locker room, and so on. In case anyone was operating on any faulty assumptions, this speech was designed to drive home one point: this endeavor these potential players were committing to would require a level of discipline and hard work that some of them had never experienced before.

The sacrifices demanded by my dad were laid out before the team, and then my dad would make the following statement every season: "So decide today if you want to be part of this team. If you don't like what will be required of you by me and our coaching staff, now is the time to leave. Sit in the stands on Fridays and tell everyone how great you would have been if I hadn't mistreated you."

This was the moment each year when there was an uncomfortable pause. The veterans would never fail to look around them to check the new guys' responses to this hard-nosed man's speech.

The new players were easy to spot; they were the young men with their eyes wide open and the undeniable look of dismay as they pondered whether they truly had what it took to play for this man. Why? Because they all knew that this coach was asking for their undivided devotion to the team. Nothing but total buy-in to the program was good enough.

It took me until I was older to realize it was all a motivational tactic. Dad was communicating his values, sure. But he was also building a brotherhood among the team. If the guys stuck with it, and almost all of them did each year, they would come out the other side stronger, closer, and a more unified team. Nothing creates a band of brothers like hard work, sacrifice, and victory.

I recall another tactic he would use to motivate us to press on. When school would let out, we would already be on the field practicing for the next game. Students would be exiting the school, books in tow, walking to the buses or their cars to head home for the day. Of course, we all knew that for us, home was still at least two and a half to three hours away.

Oftentimes, Dad would stop practice and have us watch the buses leaving, taking our classmates home. Dad's eyes would watch bus after bus before booming in that voice that required no bullhorn for amplification, "There go the 'three o'clockers,' gentleman. They don't have to worry about practice today. Look at them: they're headed home for an after-school snack and to watch TV. While you sweat and bleed, they will be in the air conditioning, drinking a Coke and eating potato chips. They are not willing to do what you are doing right now. They have no desire to switch places with you today as they look at you out the window. But come Friday night, when the lights are on, the stadium is full, the band is playing, and the cheerleaders are cheering, when you walk on the field, they will yearn to switch places with you. When that moment comes, remember that every sacrifice you are making will pale in comparison to the reward that is waiting." No one could motivate like my dad.

Now, it's certain that some of the students in the stands on Friday nights were content to be there. But there had to be a kernel of truth to what Dad said. And for us, it was all the motivation we needed to keep grinding. He made being on that field feel special in a way that's hard to describe. No matter how hard it got, to a man, all of us would rather be on the field than watching from the bleachers.

What would you say if I asked you if you would rather be on the field or in the stands? Most men reading this would likely respond, "on the field." And for most men reading this, "on the field" isn't good enough. Not only would they want to be on the field, but they'd want to be making plays and contributing to the team effort.

Maybe you're reading this, and you've never touched a football in your life. But you understand the desire to be participating versus spectating. Most of us are wired to be a part of something bigger than us. The thought of sitting in the stands, detached from the action, watching instead of contributing, would eat most of us alive. That is why it is so perplexing to me that most men don't seem to care about "participating" in the service of the Lord. When it comes to living their life on mission for Christ, many men seem content to "sit in the stands."

In the circles I travel in, men constantly make fun of the "participation trophy" culture of youth sports (and, if we're honest, of our culture in general). The participation trophy is earned simply for finishing the game or the season, regardless of how well you or your team performed. We don't want anyone's feelings to get hurt or let down. So, every team, every player, first place to last, gets a trophy. Gone are the days when excellence was rewarded and coming up short was the motivation for your next best effort. Everyone gets a trophy! It's funny to me how men will make fun of this in sports while at the same time expecting to get a "participation trophy" from Jesus for what amounts to a lackluster effort at serving Him.

Now, it's very important to point out that I am not talking about earning our salvation by our "performance." I'm not talking about a works-based faith. The Apostle Paul made it quite clear in Ephesians 2:8–9 that it is by grace we have been saved through faith. Paul reminds us that this is not our own doing but is a gift from God. Our salvation is "not a result of works, so that no one may boast." I'm not talking about a misguided theology that says God loves or saves me more because I check all the boxes and follow the rules. I'm referring to embracing what Paul mentions in Ephesians 2:10.

Immediately after Paul so powerfully assures us of our redemption through faith in Jesus, he says, "We are [God's] workmanship, created in Christ Jesus for good works, which God prepared beforehand, that we should walk in them." Apparently, this redemption in Christ (that we did not earn) is so powerful and life-changing that it produces righteous works in us. If we faithfully follow Jesus, there is an expectation that our lives will be full of good, righteous, Kingdom-advancing "works" *because* of our redemption.

Have you gone to work? Is your life overflowing with impactful, culture-changing actions? Are you making disciples? Can you teach others what Jesus commanded as He instructed all who have been redeemed? Do you model an active, authentic, meaningful faith? Let me ask this another way: Are you on the field? Or watching from the stands?

The Apostle Paul says something else very interesting in Philippians 3:13–14. Paul has just said that he doesn't think he has obtained all the spiritual growth available to Him in Christ. He says, ". . . forgetting what lies behind and straining forward to what lies ahead, I press on toward the goal for the prize of the upward call of God in Christ Jesus." I press on toward the goal for the prize of the upward call of God in Christ Jesus! Straining forward and pressing on toward the goal are strong, active words. What is Paul talking about? It isn't earning our redemption because Paul just told us we can't earn or accomplish our righteousness. So, what is he straining and pressing toward? What prize? Maybe we should look at 2 Corinthians 5:10 for our answer.

In 2 Corinthians 5, Paul is talking to the church at Corinth about the sin that has infiltrated this church. He is encouraging them to remember that they will face God in judgment one day. Paul reminds them that though only the lost will face the white throne of judgment, we all will face the judgment seat, or the "bema seat," of Jesus Christ. Why will the redeemed stand before the judgment seat of Christ? Paul explains: "For we must all appear before the judgment seat of Christ, so that each one may receive what is due for what he has done in the body, whether good or evil." We can also see similar language in Romans 14:10. Paul clearly states that Jesus isn't giving or taking salvation away. Jesus is addressing the saved. Instead, He is giving out and taking away *rewards* in heaven.

Everyone who has truly believed in the name of Jesus for salvation and has been born again by the power of the Holy Spirit will be with God in eternity. But not everyone will receive a "well done, good and faithful servant." That is the goal Paul is pursuing! Why does he care if he is already redeemed by grace through faith? Because Paul understands what Jesus Christ had to endure to redeem him from sin.

Paul is so grateful for his redemption and completely understands the cost it required that he is ready to obey his Lord and Savior, whatever cost that requires of him, not in any attempt to earn redemption, but to *show gratitude* for his redemption. Paul desires to obey his Lord and Savior because he loves Him (John 14:15). Paul wants only to know Jesus better and be with Him in eternity when his time of service is done. Why do men care so much about the applause of the world and so little about the applause of God? The reason is that too many times, men have placed more value on the first than the latter. Will you get a "well done"? Are you striving for a "well done"?

Paul ended his life completely convinced he would receive the crown of righteousness from his Lord and Savior. In 2 Timothy 4:7–8, Paul doesn't even hesitate. He says, "I have fought the good fight, I have finished the race, I have kept the faith. Henceforth there is laid up for me the crown of righteousness, which the Lord, the righteous judge, will award to me on that day, and not only to me but also to all who have loved his appearing." The day is coming when we will all face Jesus. And just like those "three o'clockers" who on game day will yearn to be on the field, those who refused to fight the good fight and keep the faith will yearn to be like the Apostle Paul.

Chapter 6
No Excuses

I actually grew up thinking that my childhood was normal. I really did. I thought it was perfectly normal for your dad to stand in the doorway of any given room on any given day in nothing but his underwear and ask his children if any of us thought we could move him from the doorway. We would run into his massive body only to collapse laughing against the mountain of a man that was my father. Over and over again. It never got old, and, again, I just assumed my other friends' dads were the same way. Of course, there was a moment when, as an adult, I realized that other people did not play this game with their dads. If you attempt it outside of your home, you end up conversing with a law enforcement or HR officer pretty quickly.

By this point, you will have no doubt come to understand that my dad was unique. He was unique in so many ways. But much of what made him unique was how exacting he was about everything. There was a right way to do things, and there was little room in his life for doing anything the wrong way. There were things he simply would not tolerate. Maybe the thing that he had the least tolerance for was excuses.

My dad loathed people who made excuses when they did not meet the expected standard. He could not abide someone making an excuse for coming up short because of a lack of effort or execution. I recall repeatedly hearing him say when someone had made an excuse for not doing their job on the field, in our home, or at school, "Stop making excuses and just tell me you did not get the job done." I can still hear him say it.

My dad wasn't ungracious or overly demanding. His intolerance of excuses wasn't about him being strict or harsh. It was way deeper than that. More than anything, Dad was concerned with ownership. An excuse was an attempt to dodge ownership. Dad wanted the individual to own the mistake, *correct* the mistake, and then move on.

We can all admit that it's hard to respect a leader who demands a standard from those in his or her charge that they themselves do not meet or even desire to meet. My dad was a great leader because he never called anyone to a standard that he didn't first hold himself to. My dad lived by the exact same standard he expected from others. When he fell short, he acknowledged it, learned from it, and moved on.

My dad coached for thirty-plus years, and, yes, he won more games than he lost. But I cannot ever recall Dad making an excuse for a loss. He might have hated officials, but I never heard him blame them for his team's loss. He never blamed the weather. He never blamed his assistant coaches. And he certainly never

ever blamed his players. He always gave credit to the opponent for getting the job done and took the responsibility for not having his team ready to win.

I vividly remember a Sunday afternoon after church. We had just finished one of my mom's famously delicious lunches. Dad and I were watching the coach's show for the team, which Dad's team had just beaten quite handily the previous day. The coach was going on about how bad the weather had been for the game. He was correct; the weather had been horrible. I remember Dad sitting in his hat, shirt, shorts, black coach's shoes, and tube socks around his ankles. Dad stood in front of the TV, listened for a moment longer, then turned to me and said, "Listening to this guy, you would think it only rained on one side of the field." Dad then turned and walked out of the room. He could stand the excuses no longer.

I remember the first time I understood my dad's insistence that we not make excuses. I was older when it finally hit me that my dad was really looking for acknowledgment that we understood what we were supposed to do and had failed to meet the standard. He did not want to hear us blame someone else. He did not want to hear that we *mostly* did what we were instructed. He just wanted to hear us say that we messed up, take responsibility for our failure, and work to avoid repeating the same mistake. I don't know about you, but this sounds an awful lot like repentance.

Repentance is a key theme in Scripture and essential to our salvation. And yet, it's not something we hear people talk about enough. But Jesus talked about it. In Matthew 4, we see Jesus coming out of His 40 days of temptation in the wilderness. Jesus, of course, had every excuse in the book to listen to the devil and give in to his suggestions. But He did not. Matthew 4:17 tells us that from the moment Jesus passed the test in the wilderness, He began His public ministry, saying, "Repent, for the kingdom of heaven is at hand." Jesus would go on in Luke 13 to preach that all who do not repent will perish.

What does repentance mean? Simple. It's a word picture. To repent means to turn 180 degrees from our sin and turn back to Jesus. To repent is to cry out to be forgiven. This call to repentance has become less and less popular in the modern Western church. We say things like, "Jesus hung out with sinners," and "Jesus meets you right where you are," etc. And, of course, it is true that Jesus did hang out with sinners and that He will meet us right where we are. But the part we don't focus enough on is that He doesn't allow us to stay where we were. He meets us as sinners but does not leave us in sin. He calls us to repentance!

Jesus meets us sinners where we are. But when Jesus leaves the company of sinners, the only people who were changed were the sinners, not Jesus. If we go to Acts 2, we will find Peter, indwelled with the Holy Spirit, preaching with such power that Luke tells us the people's hearts were cut. They were convicted, and they cried out to Peter, "What must we do!" Can I tell you what Peter did not say? "I don't know," or "God will work it out." No, Peter had been taught well by his Lord and Savior and did not hesitate to tell them what he had heard Jesus say repeatedly: you must repent. No excuses. No blame. Just pure ownership of your sin and failure to live up to God's standard.

Jesus did not go to the cross for our excuses. He became the sacrifice for our sins. We must stop attempting to justify sin in our lives and admit that we are not getting the job done. We have failed to meet the standard. We need to just admit that. We alone are the ones who have messed it all up. Own it, and then ask Jesus to forgive us, give us a second chance, and enable us to meet God's standard as only He can.

I recall a situation where I came face to face with this reality. I was leading the men's ministry of our local church, and we decided to use a faith-based movie that had just been released as an opportunity to present the Gospel to those who were attending. The plan was to buy all the tickets for three showings and give the tickets out. Then, when the movie ended, we would present the Gospel to the audience and ask for a response. Three of us volunteered to take on one theater each.

After the movie ended, we would let each other know how it went. I got a call from one of the theaters that one of the men did not show up. I called the one who did not show up, and I heard a lot of excuses. The more this man talked, the clearer it became that he simply didn't do what he said he would do. He didn't show up, and he didn't get anyone to fill in for him.

I reached a point in the conversation where I heard my dad's words coming out of my mouth. I told this individual that I would really appreciate it if he would stop making excuses, admit that he didn't do what he said he would do, and that he wouldn't do it again. Just say you didn't do what you committed to. Just tell the truth and drop the excuses. At some point, he very begrudgingly did, but I could tell there wasn't very much real ownership. Sadly,

I never tasked him with any other responsibility in our men's ministry, not because he made a mistake (we all make mistakes), but because he made excuses. He never owned it.

There is no room for excuses in true repentance. Thomas Brooks said, "Repentance is the vomit of the soul." We serve a Lord who, though He is God incarnate, lowered Himself to take the role of a servant and be obedient to the point of death, even death on a cross (Philippians 2:7–8). Jesus never asks of us anything that He hasn't already done.

It's time we stop making excuses. We are all in need of redemption. Let today be the day you accept responsibility for your sin and turn to the only one able to remove that sin from your life: Jesus.

Chapter 7
Confidence vs. Arrogance

My brother and I had the wonderful pleasure of playing for Dad in high school when he was coaching at Oxford High School in Oxford, Alabama. (Yes, I can truthfully say that my brother and I are Oxford graduates!) My brother Greg was the type of player my dad loved. My brother was smaller than me but was vicious. Dad often told me, "If your brother had your size, they would outlaw him."

My brother used every ounce of strength to destroy whomever he was tackling. Greg played defensive back and I played defensive tackle. My work ethic at practice was questionable at best and I did seem to carry a sense of what I called "confidence." My dad would often disagree with my assessment and let me know clearly that there was a fine line between confidence and arrogance. Dad often felt I confused the two.

My dad was a very good football coach. His inductions into various Halls of Fame, both on the high school and collegiate level, affirm this truth. However, Dad was as humble a man as I have ever known. Now, let me be clear: as we have established, my dad believed he could whip any man alive. This is a fact. But he would say that was confidence, not arrogance. Nothing made him more uncomfortable than when it came to accolades and pats on the back. When asked to comment on an award or an achievement, he would say things like, "You know, the years I had great players, I seemed to be a much better coach." Dad understood humility.

Two stories sum up Dad's professional humility. One involves a salesman who called on Dad one day to sell him some football equipment. The salesman told me that he couldn't find my dad one day when he arrived at the athletic department. He began to search for my dad in the locker room but couldn't find him anywhere. When he eventually found him, my dad was in the bathroom cleaning the toilets. Understand that at the time, Dad was the head football coach and the athletic director. The salesman told me that when he asked Dad why in the world he was cleaning the toilets, my dad simply replied, "Because it's my turn." Did you hear that answer? No wonder men would follow my dad into battle. Though Dad was clearly in charge, he never asked anyone to do anything he wasn't willing to do. As a leader, do you take your turn cleaning the toilets?

The next story was when Dad was coaching college football at Jacksonville State University. After three trips to the Division II National Championship, the Gamecocks won the Championship in 1992 by knocking down a last-minute fourth down throw to the end zone by Pittsburg State. When the game was over, a reporter asked Dad if he had called the defensive coverage that had led to the victory. My dad's answer showed his humility. He responded to the reporter by asking his own question. "So let me ask you a question," my dad said. "If the national championship were on the line, who would you let make the call: The defensive coordinator who has watched dozens of hours of film on the opposing offense's tendencies or the guy who spoke this week at the Rotary Club luncheon?" Dad had every opportunity to take credit for the win but used the moment to elevate someone else's efforts. I can honestly tell you that in the same situation, I don't know many head coaches who would have done the same thing then or now. Dad taught me so much about humility, and sadly, the times I didn't listen, I paid the price.

Dad always used terms that were as unique as him. I recall him saying that he did not like working with "I" people. I remember the first time he brought this up, and I thought he was talking about "eye" people. It was confusing because I didn't know what an "eye" person looked like. Was this some form of half-human, half-cyclops creature? Of course, Dad was talking about the pronoun, not the part of the human body that gives us sight.

Dad didn't trust people who would talk about what *they* had done versus talking about what the entire staff and team had done. We have all heard these people who say, "I called some good plays today," or "I put us in a good position to win the game," or "My game plan worked really well," and so on. Dad said he preferred "we" people over "I" people. "We prepared well this week," "We made tackles when we needed to stop our opponent," or "I thought the game plan 'we' put together was executed well by the players."

Dad believed that "I" people lay awake at night thinking of ways to get you beat. "I" people think the rules and expectations of the team don't apply to them. They believe they are the center of the universe and have somehow accomplished these things independently. Dad loved football because he said that it was the ultimate team sport. "I" people have a hard time in the game of football because it requires "we" to win. The players have to buy into the program and system and surrender their selfishness to succeed. Dad loved the game and claimed that it had no equal because it forced people to give up themselves for the good of the overall team. If someone did not agree with this philosophy, they would not be long for any of Dad's teams or staff.

The Bible has a wonderful story of a classic "I" man. And we get to see God deal with him in a mighty way. King Nebuchadnezzar had an arrogance problem, and God had to deal with it. Daniel 4 tells us that no matter how often God revealed Himself to the king, ole Nebuchadnezzar seemed to always become full of himself and drift back into his old pagan ways. Daniel 4:4 says, "I, Nebuchadnezzar, was at ease in my house and prospering in my palace." Yup, there's an "I" man if I've ever seen one.

Please don't miss the words "ease" and "prospering" in this verse. The King is "knocking it out of gear" and reflecting on his victories and wealth. There's nothing wrong with taking it easy, and there's nothing wrong with wealth unless we forget to give credit to the one who provides all we have and the ability to accomplish all we may accomplish. God knows our hearts, and He knew Nebuchadnezzar's. God, in His grace, sent the king a dream to warn him that he was about to be humbled.

Has God ever sent warnings into your life that you ignored? I wish I could say "no," but I must admit that He has sent warnings to me that I ignored. Daniel, always ready to step in and attest to God's greatness, lets the king know that this dream is a warning from God that the king is about to be humbled if he doesn't change from an "I" person to a "we" person. God gives Nebuchadnezzar a year to adjust. But sadly for the king, he didn't heed the warning. How many times have we all seen this in ourselves or others that we love? This is why accountability only works if we listen to the warnings of those who can see what we are missing.

Daniel 4:29 tells us that after twelve months, King Nebuchadnezzar was really impressed with the magnificence of Babylon, which, according to history, was something to behold. The hanging gardens of Babylon alone were said to be one of the wonders of the ancient world. The king conquered all his foes with victory after victory, and his wealth was unmatched. But did the king thank God for allowing him to build such a beautiful, prosperous kingdom? No, Nebuchadnezzar took all the credit with a big "look at everything I have done."

Nebuchadnezzar's arrogance was about to receive a reality check. Daniel 4:30 tells us that the king was walking on the roof, looking at his kingdom and his palace, and saying, "Is not this great Babylon, which I have built by my mighty power as a royal residence and for the glory of my majesty?" That was all God needed to hear, and He took it away from the king.

God allowed Nebuchadnezzar to feel the full weight of His discipline. As soon as Nebuchadnezzar boasted about his greatness, everything changed: "While the words were still in the king's mouth, there fell a voice from heaven, 'O King Nebuchadnezzar, to you it is spoken: The kingdom has departed from you, and you shall be driven from among men, and your dwelling shall be with the beasts of the field. And you shall be made to eat grass like an ox, and seven periods of time shall pass over you, until you know that the Most High rules the kingdom of men and gives it to whom he will.'" Immediately the word was fulfilled against Nebuchadnezzar" (Daniel 4:31–33). For seven years, the great king was reduced to living like an ox, eating grass, and sleeping on the ground.

God is really good at humbling "I" people, in part because He will not share His glory with anyone or anything. We must remember that there is nothing that we have or receive that didn't come from God. He has given us every talent and every blessing. And any reward or accolade we receive is only because He gave us the ability to earn it.

Ultimately, the goal of every man should be to use the gifts that God has given us to glorify Him, not ourselves. He loves us enough to humble us if we aren't willing to do so on our own. As I write this book, I have been doing a nationally syndicated radio show for several decades. If I haven't used the gifts and the platform that God has given me to glorify Him and advance His Kingdom (not mine), it has been a monumental waste of time.

My dad wasn't a perfect man, not by any stretch. But he was a good example of what it meant to be a man—not a perfect example, but a very good one. There is only one example of perfect manhood, and that is when God became one. Have you ever thought about that before? God became a man. Fully God and fully man, He took on human flesh, was tempted by everything we have been tempted with, and did not sin.

Jesus modeled many things for us, not the least of which is leadership. He showed us that proper leadership is His humble leadership; He washed the feet of those He had authority over. He showed us that proper leadership is servant leadership; He never asked any of us to do anything He hadn't already done for us. When He commanded us to deny ourselves, count the cost, pick up our cross, and take on a difficult path, He did every one of those things first. He led by example, not just words.

True repentance requires humility. We must be humble enough to acknowledge we are sinners in need of God's grace. James 4:6 says, "But he gives more grace. Therefore, it says, "God opposes the proud but gives grace to the humble." This isn't a very popular posture these days. Arrogance and self-promotion have become not only accepted but encouraged. James 4:10 similarly reminds us to humble ourselves before the Lord, and He will exalt us. James is making the point that if we want to be lifted up by God, we must first be humble enough to admit we are nothing but wretched sinners in desperate need of God's grace and mercy.

Humility is so important that the apostle Paul says in 2 Corinthians 12:7–9 that God gave him a thorn in his flesh to keep him from becoming conceited. Paul even pleaded with God for the thorn to be removed, but God did not remove it because God knew that Paul needed it so that he would remain humble. Paul actually said the Lord said no to his request for the thorn to leave him. But Paul isn't confused about why God would not remove the thorn: "But he said to me, 'My grace is sufficient for you, for my power is made perfect in weakness.' Therefore I will boast all the more gladly of my weaknesses, so that the power of Christ may rest upon me" (2 Corinthians 12:9). Paul goes on to say in response to this truth that he boasts in his weakness so that the power of Christ may rest upon him. If that is not a powerful understanding of why God humbles us, I don't know what it is.

Are you willing to be weak to be strong? Don't miss that God loved Paul enough to give him the thorn. Humility is so crucial to accessing the power of Christ that God will do whatever it takes to humble us, even allowing us to suffer. Are you willing to humble yourself? No matter how much the world may celebrate arrogance, God opposes the proud. Maybe today is the day for us to finally accept that.

Chapter 8
Be Perfect

My dad sought perfection in every team he coached. He truly believed that if his teams did enough reps and worked hard enough, they could master their technique and reach the goal of perfection. Coach Bill Burgess demanded flawless execution in every phase of the greatest game ever created.

Now is as good a time as any in this recollection of my dad to digress from this story to mention his belief that American Football was the greatest game ever conceived. The converse of this is also true: my dad believed that European Football, or soccer, was the worst game ever created. He truly hated the game of soccer until the day that he left this earth. Not only did he dislike it as an actual game, but he was certain it was a communist plot to sow seeds of rot deep within the United States.

When Dad was the athletic director at Oxford High School, he resolutely opposed the onset of soccer in our country, forbidding soccer to infiltrate his beloved athletic department. Against the demands of a few voices in our city that Oxford High School form a soccer team, Bill Burgess stood tall and would not allow a team to be formed.

Years later, after Dad retired from coaching and long after soccer was a varsity sport at Oxford High School (and essentially every other high school in the country), we were relaxing on the beach during a family vacation. As Dad and I were discussing the topics of the day, I noticed a man with a ponytail kicking a soccer ball a good distance down the beach. Unfortunately for all of us, he was headed our way.

Watching this man approach us, I began to anticipate his arrival with dread. I was no longer even listening to what Dad was talking about anymore. I watched Dad's eyes as they scanned the beautiful Gulf of Mexico until the moment those dark brown eyes, which you could barely see under my dad's granite brow, locked on the ponytail-wearing soccer enthusiast. With every kick, kick, kick of the forbidden ball, it was as if the man "kicked, kicked, kicked" away the joy of our surroundings.

Like a sentry on a wall, Dad's head turned slowly from left to right with the rhythm of the ponytailed Pele's kicking as he first came abreast and then passed us. Dad's gaze followed him all the way to the extreme right, staring the whole time with what could only be described as a snarl until the man was far enough away for Dad to feel OK facing forward again. Crisis averted. Threat minimized.

As I snuck a glimpse at Dad out of my peripheral vision, I saw him once again staring at the greenish blue water of the Gulf, his eyes fixed forward on the day's sunset, the beautiful waves lapping the sand at our feet. After a moment of silence, in his powerful voice, louder than the breeze and the waves, Dad said, "Do you remember when people got upset when I said that soccer would destroy this country?" I replied, "Yes, Dad. Yes, I do." To which my dad replied with a timing that would be the envy of any comedian, "Does anybody want to give me an apology?" Bill Burgess was a modern-day Paul Revere when it came to soccer, yet he knew his warning would likely be unheeded. Dad, you were right. We did not listen. But back to the subject of perfection, about which my dad also had strong opinions.

Dad was raised in the church by his parents. His mother's name was Margaret Burgess. We called her MeMaw, an endearing nickname many Southerners use for our grandmothers. She was a powerful woman of God involved in every aspect of the local church. She taught Sunday school, worked with the youth (or, as she called them, the "young people"), sang in the choir, played the bells in the handbell choir, and served on more committees than one could count. William Calvin Burgess, or as we called him PawPaw (yet another southern nickname for granddads), was a bit more laid back and could be mischievous. PawPaw's friends called him Shorty Burgess. We think this was due to the fact that he was actually pretty tall for the time period in which he grew up. Dad was greatly influenced by them both. And though Dad was redeemed by his faith in Jesus, like all of us, he was a work in progress. I had to wait until MeMaw went to heaven before I could tell or write about my dad's struggles with his language.

Dad was never profane but could use language his mother would not have approved of, and he was determined to work on it. Dad had a paddle wrapped in athletic tape in his office that he used to correct both his players and his sons. My brother and I had to avoid this paddle in athletics and at home. The paddle usually got to ride shotgun from the office to the house on any given report card day. I will be forever grateful for my parents loving me enough to discipline me, and my dad was very good at "discipline via paddle." It was so good that he rarely had to use it. The thought of it alone kept many a young man (and a young Burgess) walking the line. When my dad administered the paddle, he knew how to make it count.

In 1982, I was playing football for Dad at Oxford High School and was fortunate enough to be voted by my teammates to be one of the team's four captains. The tradition was two captains for offense and two captains for defense. That year, Dad did something profound: He decided that he would allow the team captains to hold him accountable concerning his language on the field. This would lead to one of the most epic encounters of my adolescence.

I can still remember the day my dad stood before the team and gave a speech about this new authority he was giving to the team captains. We were standing in a group, and Dad began to talk to us about his use of colorful language and his desire to correct this behavior. Dad proceeded to set out the accountability he would subject himself to for violating his new rules on language. What came out of his mouth is still surprising to me today. Dad said that if he used inappropriate language during practice or a game, the team captains would hold him accountable by giving him a lick with his own paddle. The room was suddenly silent.

I must be honest: Dad had initiated these attempts before, so I was tuning him out. I wasn't paying attention until I heard the team gasp. One of my teammates, whom I had known since we were in the second grade, grabbed my arm as if he couldn't believe what he was hearing. The man whom we all feared and respected had just given permission for members of the team to paddle him. He had taken this further by including me in the select few people who could paddle him. What was happening?

At that moment, I didn't know what to think. I didn't know what to say. I didn't know what to do. A wide range of different emotions overwhelmed me. Was I seriously going to get an opportunity to paddle the man who had paddled me my whole life? Was that allowed? I loved my dad and respected him, but at the same time, I knew he wouldn't make it very long until someone would be paddling him. Would that person be me?

I went over to the other three captains, who were just as shaken up and confused as I was. The team began to file onto the practice field. We barely had time to take it in. We wondered what would happen if he cussed today in practice. Who would do the deed? In order to minimize worlds colliding, we quickly decided that our star running back, Gerald Wayne McRath, would be first up, and I would be moved to the fourth and final spot. They knew that I needed time to process this rare gift, test, curse, or whatever this opportunity was.

As predicted, Dad made it about a practice and a half before he violated his new standard. When practice ended, we all hurried off the field to go to the locker room to see what would happen. Dad did not hesitate to bring out the feared paddle and put it into the hands of Gerald Wayne. We all wondered what his play would be. Would he let Dad have a good one or go easy on him? How would this coach, whom we all feared, react? How much rope had Dad really given us? Was this, after all, a trick?

Gerald Wayne was holding the paddle. Dad turned and faced the wall, assuming the position countless other players had assumed before. Would any of our lives ever be the same? McRath took no chances and placed that paddle against my dad's rear end with so little force it wouldn't have broken an egg. The team responded with silence. There was literally no reaction. We were all so confused. If we booed, would this bring fury? If we cheered, would he see us as weak and afraid? My dad was perpetrating a mind game like no other.

Gerald Wayne returned the paddle to Dad and went to his locker, relieved that this opportunity/test/curse was over. As I watched my childhood friend walk away, I began to sense disappointment rising inside of me. Where was McRath's gentleness coming from? Dad would have never given us that type of merciful pat! He had his shot, and he squandered it!

Dad never brought work home. He was Dad at home and Coach on the field. He never mixed the two worlds. We never had any issues with the overbearing coach/dad, who talked about practice or the game at home and took us outside and made us do drills, etc. This was not who he was, and I am grateful that my dad masterfully balanced these two roles. But at dinner that night, I sensed he was wondering what I would do if he continued to stumble and offer me the same opportunity that Gerald Wayne had squandered. We never spoke of this at home, but deep down, we both knew the day was coming when I would have the paddle in my hand.

Within the next two weeks, Bruce Harmon and Robby Bussey both had their opportunity to paddle Dad, and both took the Gerald Wayne McRath approach: tiny baby taps of the paddle, much more symbolic than punishing. My three fellow captains had taken the road of least resistance. Now, all eyes were on me.

The entire team knew we would not get to mid-season before the bell would toll for me. And as fate would have it, the fateful day came on a Tuesday in early October. We could sense that the coaching staff was growing increasingly irritated by what they deemed our lack of effort. Then it happened, the most forbidden of all sins: a fumble.

My dad hated fumbling like my mother hates rats. Dad truly believed that no one should ever fumble. Now would be a good time to note that Dad also believed his players should never have cramps. My dad may be the only coach ever documented to forbid cramps. Every player who ever played for Bill Burgess knew that if he came on the field to get you only to find out you had cramps, your playing opportunities would diminish greatly. Dad was on record for hating fumbling and cramps.

On this October day, not only did our offense fumble, but our defense did not recover the fumble. If you have ever seen a rocket on the launching pad, you know when it's about to take off. Smoke begins to billow out from under the thrusters. You know it will be leaving the launching pad very soon. We looked at Dad's black coaching shoes, complete with the tube socks around the ankles, and we could almost see the smoke coming from underneath. Shockingly, he seemed like he was holding it together. That is, until the offense scored on the very next play. This was too much for Dad.

Dad exploded into a tirade, aimed first at the offense for fumbling in the first place, then at the defense (his first love) for failing to recover the forbidden fumble and doubling down on the missed opportunity by letting the offense score on the next play. Then it happened. Dad began to describe to the defense what the offense just did to us with the ball as an object lesson. He held the ball in such a way that we all knew that what Dad would say would not only be anatomically impossible but would most definitely violate his new commitment to removing cussing from his language.

As a team, we had heard Dad use this analogy before, but on this particular day, some extra words were added for emphasis that, had we known ahead of time, we would have found something with which to write them down for future reference. Dad had done it. He had once again violated his new standard on swearing. The day had come. When and if this practice ended, I would face one of the biggest decisions in my young life. I would soon be holding my dad's paddle with full permission to give my dad a lick.

As we all jogged to the dressing room that evening, the anticipation on the team was reaching a fever pitch. My brother Greg was on the team that year, the only year that he and I played on the same team. It was a special season. For the first and only time, Mom had both of her sons and her husband on the same team together, and now here I was about to paddle not just my coach but my dad. My younger brother Greg didn't know what to do with the scene about to play out before us all. Does he distance himself from me? Does he stand in solidarity with me? After all, we had both been paddled by this man; this was our shot, right? I resolved that I would do this not just for myself but also for my baby brother.

Dad got right to it. As soon as we got in the dressing room, he handed me the paddle, announced that he had violated his new standard, and stated that it was time for him to take his lick. I had removed my shoulder pads and stood in my football pants and cut-off undershirt, drenched in sweat from practice. Dad turned against the wall and provided the target. No one said a word. And then everything seemed to go in slow motion. I gripped the paddle, fully extended my right arm above my head, twisted my torso, set my jaw, and then . . . . At that precise moment, it was as if I had left my body and was watching myself from afar, almost as if it was too late to stop. I couldn't believe it, but I swung so hard that I actually took a slight "crow hop" before delivering the blow. The force of the lick from the paddle lifted Dad to his toes as the echo of the blow reverberated through the room. There was a moment of silence as coaches, trainers, water boys, and players could not believe what had just happened. I had decided to flip the script.

My teammates had all decided to take the easy way out, but was that working? No? Coach Burgess asked for someone to hold him accountable, and though it might have been an unpleasant job, I was the man to do it.

Dad left the locker room without a word and went into his office. Once the team was sure he was gone, they began to give me a variety of responses. Some celebrated, some were terrified, others were confused. No one knew exactly how to respond. My brother seemed more curious than anything. I think he wondered if this would be the incident that would truly test Dad's commitment to never bring work home.

I took a shower and put back on my school clothes. As we prepared to leave, some teammates of mine seemed to think they should distance themselves from me after the shocking incident. Dressed, I started for the car, but I had a moment of hesitation. You had to go by my dad's office to leave the field house. That day, I wanted nothing more than to scurry past the office to the parking lot unnoticed. But just as I was about to pass his door, I noticed it was open. It was time to face the piper.

As I knew it would, I heard the booming voice call out to me. I turned to stand in the doorway. "Did you enjoy that?" Dad said. Sensing an opportunity I may never have again, I replied in my most adult voice, trying not to smirk, "I was just doing what you asked us to do. To hold you accountable. You don't know how much that hurt me to have to do that today, but as much as it hurt, I did it because I love you and want the best for you." My reply caused a sly smile to creep across my dad's face. He looked at me and said, "It's a long season, Son. I sure hope that you can be perfect when it comes to following team rules. I hope you don't mess up and break one. See you at home." I turned to walk away, heart pounding in my chest. As I pushed open the double doors leading into the parking lot, I mumbled, "Rick, what have you just done."

You know, perfection was a topic Jesus didn't shy away from. During the Sermon on the Mount, Jesus reminded those in attendance that the only way to be in the presence of our perfect heavenly Father is to also be perfect. Why was Jesus telling them, and by default us, that we must be perfect? Because that is the standard.

Jesus clearly states in Matthew 5:48, "You therefore must be perfect, as your heavenly Father is perfect." God is flawless and holy, perfect in all His attributes. But we are not. We are imperfect and rebellious. Jesus is making the point that for God to link Himself in relationship with any other party, that party must also be perfect. If that weren't the case, God would violate His perfection by merely associating with something imperfect. And His perfection is an aspect of His nature that is unchanging. He can never *not* be perfect. It doesn't take long to realize that this is a standard we can never attain.

God's standard of perfection is unattainable for humans. Unattainable, that is, without the sacrifice that Jesus provides. This is the bad news (unattainable standard) that leads to the good news (Jesus as the means of attaining perfection). In the past, I have heard well-meaning preachers and teachers say that we don't have to be perfect to go to heaven. While I understand their heart, it's simply not true. The standard of spending eternity with God is perfection. But the beautiful news of the Gospel is that Jesus accomplishes this standard on our behalf.

Jesus went to the cross to meet God's qualifying standard of perfection for anyone willing to repent of their sins, leave their faith in themselves, and place their faith fully in Jesus. Why? Because it's Jesus and only Jesus that makes us fully righteous, fully perfect. When we come to faith in Jesus, God, in His great mercy, is pleased to take the righteousness of Jesus and apply it to us (Colossians 1:21–23). Jesus doesn't make the redeemed partially righteous; He makes them fully righteous and fully acceptable to our Heavenly Father. This is the theological concept of justification at work.

Paul spells this out clearly in his letter to the Ephesians. In Ephesians 2:8–9, he says, "For by grace you have been saved through faith. And this is not your own doing; it is the gift of God, not a result of works, so that no one may boast." We are justified and made perfect by God's grace through faith in Jesus, not faith in our ability to live perfectly. Justification is all in the work of Jesus. He provided the sacrifice demanded by a Holy God.

Jesus took upon Himself the holy wrath God directs at sin so that all who repent and place their faith in Jesus' finished work on the cross might be justified. Once justified, we begin our sanctification (the process of being made holy), which does require action on our part. We are called to abide in Jesus (see John 15), study the Word of God, pray, worship, serve, and so on. Sanctification continues until we are glorified either at our earthly death or the return of Christ. The ongoing battle between our sinful nature will finally be over when we are glorified. Only then will we be perfect, all made possible by God's love and mercy.

We must stop trying to devise a game plan to be perfect or to appear perfect through our own efforts. This only leads to frustration. Repent, submit to Jesus' authority, abide in Him, and be made perfect in God's eyes through Jesus.

My dad was right, in a way: Perfection *is* the standard. But only Jesus provides the power to meet that standard.

Chapter 9
Fear

My dad coached high school football for the first twenty years of my life. Some of my fondest memories are playing for him in the early 1980s. One thing we all knew was that Coach Burgess was the ultimate authority and was not to be crossed. I knew this all too well, being his son. I was already well-versed in how he felt about authority.

I will never forget growing up in a little house in a neighborhood called Cheaha Acres #1. Our home was nestled in the valley of Cheaha Mountain, the highest point in my home state of Alabama. (The term Cheaha comes from the Creek Indian language and means "high place.") Not too far from ours was a neighborhood that was our backyard football rival. It was creatively named Cheaha Acres #2.

Our little house wasn't fancy, but it was ours. We had a gravel driveway, and when I think back, I don't know anyone who had a garage. We all had carports, which were nothing more than concrete slabs with coverings over them, open on two sides so you could pull your car out of the rain. My brother Greg and I shared a room until we both left home. In our room were two twin beds and two dressers in which we kept our clothes. On top of the dressers were our various Little League trophies. Greg and I got along great but found our fair share of mischief.

My brother and I were raised to respect our parents, and we did, but trouble seemed to find us almost every day. When it came to being disciplined, Dad was rarely called in for the daily stuff. Mom would usually handle the small stuff like a fight, not cleaning our rooms, breaking something, trouble with neighborhood kids, etc. When we got in trouble, we got spankings. Our parents didn't utilize "timeouts," unless you count us asking mom if she'd take one in the middle of whipping us with one of my dad's belts. Dad was only called in on the bigger stuff, like trouble at school, accidentally stealing plywood from a building site to build a treehouse (we thought it was leftover), shooting birds out of a neighbor's feeder with our BB guns, using the metal from the TV antenna that fell off the roof in a storm to sword fight, or, the worst offense, being disrespectful to Mom. These types of offenses were grounds for calling in Dad.

When mom would play the "Dad card," we knew we were doomed. "Well, boys, I will have to tell your dad about this when he gets home." Each time she'd say a version of those words, we'd respond the same: "Mom, no! We promise we will never do (fill in the blank) again!" Mom never did allow us to talk her out of it. My brother and I would sit on our twin beds with the NFL bedspreads with matching pillowcases and wait for Dad to come home.

When I was a boy, Dad drove a gold Chevy pickup truck. Our driveway had a drop-off from the road to the gravel. I loved that gravel driveway. I loved throwing the pieces of gravel up, hitting them with a stick far into the trees, and carving out a racetrack for my Matchbox and Hot Wheels cars. But the gravel didn't always bring joy. The sound of Dad's tires on the gravel on the days Mom had decided to bring in the big guns was a sound of dread. How could she sell us out? This same woman who made us sandwiches and Kool-Aid just a few hours before had now turned on the little boys she had claimed to love. The door of the truck would close, the sound of his shoes could be heard on the cement of the carport, the opening of the door into the kitchen from the carport, and then the sound of our mother's voice, still obviously angry with our current offense. Then, there would be a cruel silence before we'd hear the heavy steps toward our room.

My dad walked so heavily; it was as if he wore shoes made of cast iron. His every step was so solid, we would watch the trophies on our dresser rattling from the shock waves from this giant walking down the hall. Our door would open, and the sound of his authoritative voice would fill the room. If we had truly crossed a line, it would be the paddle or the belt. Whatever he chose, it would be swift and effective. We would receive the deserved correction. Why? Because my dad made it clear that he loved us enough to discipline us, to mold our characters, and to teach us to respect authority. No one enjoys discipline in the moment. But to this day, I love him for deeming me worthy of the effort.

When I joined the varsity, I knew that not following my dad's rules and expectations was not worth the price I would pay, but I just seemed to have the type of personality that needed to be corrected occasionally. A high school teacher once corrected me for making wisecracks in the classroom. She told me in front of the class that she wished me luck finding a job that would pay me to make wisecracks and make people laugh. About 15 years ago, I saw this teacher while she was out shopping, and I asked her if she had ever listened to my radio show. She looked at me like she could paddle me again and replied that yes, she had, and listening to it made her want to run her car into a ditch. She then asked me not to tell anyone that she had taught me English. But I digress.

Here I was, playing for Dad on the varsity squad. I played defensive tackle and tended to be penalized more than Dad desired. The worst offense was to be penalized on third down as the penalty would result in an unearned first down for the opposing team. In one particular game, I felt the offensive lineman was holding me, and on third down, I mentioned this to the official. I told him that I understood it might be challenging for him to see it because he was blind. I may have emphasized his condition with a word my mother wouldn't have approved of. I thought I was being empathetic. The referee disagreed.

When the flag was thrown, I heard my dad ask the official about the call. The official told my loving father that he had a personal foul on number seventy-five for cussing the referee. Dad then told the head official that he knew my mother and that I would not use that language. The referee disagreed and marked off fifteen yards. I was quickly removed from the field to face Coach Burgess.

My dad had so many cousins you couldn't count them all. My grandfather had eleven brothers and sisters, so my dad's cousins were everywhere. When I got to the sideline, Dad had a monologue for me that, though it featured some choice language of his own, was so effective I don't think I said a cussword for at least ten years. Not only was he effective, he was loud. So loud that a woman standing by the fence near the sideline heard the exchange and was appalled. "Well," she said, "he wouldn't talk to my son like that!" Leaning on the fence not far from her was one of Dad's many cousins, who looked at her and said, "That is his son."

My senior year was a doozy, as, for the first time, my little brother and I started together on the same team with Dad as head coach. It was a magical year. I will never forget that season. The memories our family made that year are deeply rooted, but there was one specific memory that I can't imagine I'll ever forget.

Dad had very specific taste. He liked what he liked and despised what he didn't. One of the things on the "despised" list was Jello. Oh, yes, He hated Jello. He often said he did not care to eat food that jiggled. His disdain for soccer has already been noted. But another thing Dad hated were players who were, in his words, "hot dogs," that is, players who showed off after a successful play. He did not allow celebrating or dancing of any kind after big plays or touchdowns. This was *strictly* forbidden. During my senior year, I would put this rule to the test.

The year was 1982. It was the Homecoming game, another thing my dad hated almost as much as Jello and dancing in the end zone. He hated all the distractions of Homecoming, the stuff other people would call "fun." The homecoming festivities drove him mad.

The practices during Homecoming week were horrible. The opponent was usually inferior, and he ensured we would not come out flat and play poorly. We practiced like it was the playoffs. He would threaten to cancel the parade, the dance, or the halftime Homecoming Queen ceremony. "Homecoming won't mean anything if we don't win the game," he would shout repeatedly during practice.

So, in 1982, a defensive tackle's dream came true on Homecoming. Every defensive lineman who has ever played the game of football dreams of scoring a touchdown. This is so extremely rare. Only the smallest percentage ever experience this thrill, but that night, ole #75 would join the ranks of the fortunate few.

Here's the scenario: It was fourth down; we had the opposing team backed up to their own thirty-yard line in punt formation. The ball is snapped and I turn away to make the wall to hopefully spring our punt returner for a good return. Then, I hear the sound: thud! It was the sound of the punt being blocked by our defensive end. I turned, and suddenly, everything seemed like it was in slow motion. I saw the football bouncing toward the end zone. I started running for the ball. As I am about to reach it, it bounces perfectly into my hands. And suddenly, just like that, I had the football. The rarest of realities for a defensive tackle had come true. Now, I had to determine what to do with it.

I harkened back to my days as an unstoppable offensive weapon in the NFL (Neighborhood Football League) when I played for the Cheaha Acres #1 Warriors. I was bigger and faster than the other kids in the neighborhood at that time and all but unstoppable. That is until I got to organized football and became a lineman. Like every lineman who has ever played, I always thought I was being held back and could have helped the team if they let me play some offense and got me the ball. This was my chance. And so began my legendary seven-yard run to the end zone on behalf of linemen everywhere.

I ran toward the front corner of the goal line and dove inside the orange pylon. As I rolled on my back, I could see the referee, Tommy, who worked at the local tire shop and refereed part-time, holding up his hands to signal that I had done it; I had actually scored a touchdown. The team rushed over. I saw my brother grinning from ear to ear, I heard the crowd going wild, and I heard the band break into our fight song. It was suddenly too much for me to take. With little forethought, I pushed everyone back and began to dance. That's right: Coach Bill Burgess' son began to dance in the end zone.

It really was something. Looking back, I showed incredible rhythm and grace as I began to rock and swing my hips with the beat of the drums. I was momentarily distracted when I saw one and then another yellow penalty flag fly in the air for unsportsmanlike conduct and delay of game (because now many of my teammates from the sidelines had also joined in). But as I trotted to the sidelines, still euphoric over this most remarkable turn of events, I began to experience a creeping uneasiness: What would my dad do?

Strangely, Dad said nothing. What was he doing? Was he going to let this go? What kind of Jedi mind trick was he pulling? Surely, he would say something. But then the game ended, we went to the dance and went home. And still, I waited. Nothing. When I woke the next morning, I expected a confrontation. But

Dad was at the office preparing for the next week's game, as usual. Would Mom say something? But, no, she seemed fine and proud of the win. By Saturday afternoon, I had convinced myself that I would get away with this moment of creative expression. We went to church Sunday morning, and still no mention of the dance.

When Dad coached at Oxford, it was tradition to meet at 2 o'clock on Sunday afternoon to review the Friday night's game film and hear the scouting report for the next opponent. There was a moment of worry for me, wondering if the film breakdown would be where he addressed my violation of his standards on celebrating, but I had just about convinced myself that I was in the clear. I had almost convinced myself that Dad had finally learned to enjoy Homecoming. I had begun to believe that my dance was so good that he found himself open to the possibility of his players having more freedom of expression. Oh, how wrong I was.

The film session started, and there was nothing out of the ordinary until we got to the punt block. As he rolls the film, Dad sets it up by saying, "Here we go. Got them backed up to their own endzone. Great job blocking the punt. Nice recovery for the score." Usually, after a touchdown, the film goes right to the extra point try, but not this time. I think what happened was that the crew recording the game assumed this would have been a special moment for our family. Smitty, who was the main camera operator, surely meant well when he decided to keep filming as I began my dance.

Back then, Dad had a button that he could use to stop the projector and run it back in order to point out anything we did right or wrong during a game. That little button could bring joy or correction. I kept waiting and hoping the video would cut away for the extra point, but in his excitement, Smitty recorded the entire dance. I was about only two hip sways in when the button stopped my dance mid-thrust. The team had begun to laugh. Maybe they were under the same delusion I was that the rules had suddenly been relaxed. Nothing could be farther from the truth. The moment of reckoning was upon us.

We never got to see the rest of my dance, and to this day, I have not seen it in its entirety. The projector was turned off, the lights turned on, and the lecture began. It featured questions like, "Do you find bush league stuff like this funny?" (By the way, no one was honest because no one said yes.) We were lectured on how that type of garbage could get us beat in a close game against a better opponent. Dad reminded us that the dance cost us not one but two penalties.

Dad was wound up. If it had been a really good team and the game had been close, I likely would not have danced, but it didn't seem like the time to point this out. I still felt like I had gotten off relatively easily; after all, I was somewhat used to the tongue-lashing. But I then learned at the same time as the rest of my teammates that after the meeting, I would join Dad on the track and run sprints and stadiums until I lost my desire to dance again. Ever. He would prove to be correct. After that afternoon with Dad at the track, I never danced on a field again, and not just because I am Southern Baptist.

In 1985, Dad's high school career came to a close and he was offered the head coaching job at Jacksonville State University.

The Gamecocks had fallen on rough times and they were looking for a coach that could return the football program to its former glory. I was offered an opportunity to work with the broadcast team, which gave me an invitation to the weekly press conference.

Dad was an old-school football coach and always clung to the notion that he was hired to win football games, not be a fundraiser. For the last fourteen years, Dad had been twelve miles south of JSU at Oxford High School, where he would sometimes go hunting prior to getting to the office in the mornings. College football was a whole new game, with an expectation to hold press conferences, go to fundraisers, and even recruit. This would all be new for Dad, and people wondered how he would handle it. But at his first press conference, Dad would set the record straight on one thing that would never change.

The school's athletic director introduced Dad, and my dad followed the introduction with some remarks of his own, as was customary. There were reporters there, and at the end of Dad's statement, they were allowed to ask questions. It didn't take long for the tone of the press conference to become apparent.

The reporter's first question to the brand-new coach was about the transition from high school to college. The reporter asked, "Coach Burgess, what are you planning to do differently now that you are coaching college versus high school?" I prepared myself, as I knew that the reporter had essentially just drawn a line in the sand. True to form, my dad stared at the reporter for a beat and then replied, "I don't fully understand your question."

The reporter took this opportunity to educate my dad. He informed Dad that he surely couldn't expect to run the program the same way it was done at Oxford High School. He pointed out how the players my dad coached lived in his community and played in the program from junior high to varsity. He noted that the kids in the Oxford school system knew Dad and his program. The reporter then apparently thought that this new coach needed to be informed that college football doesn't work that way.

"Coach," the reporter said, "these players will come from all across the country. How are you going to handle partial qualifiers? (Jacksonville State was a Division II school at this time, which meant they could accept "partial qualifiers." These players didn't have the grades to get into college or were kicked off a Division I team. They could play for a Division II school for one season. If they proved they could meet the academic requirements, they got to stay for their entire eligibility.) These will be players who don't know anything about you or your success in high school. These players could come from all over the country and have different backgrounds. Are you saying that you plan to run a college team like your high school team? What will you do to get these players to perform?"

I'll never forget the look on Dad's face: impassive. He let the young reporter get out everything he had to say, finishing his question, which had turned into a monologue. Dad began to rub his hands together as if he were warming them over a fire. I had seen this move many times throughout my life and knew this was a sign that Dad was about to set the record straight. What he said to the reporter silenced the room and set the tone for his program at JSU: "I will build my program on the foundation that it has always been built on: fear. I will ensure that no matter who they are or where they come from, every player on this team will fear me. Unless they fear my authority, it will be impossible for them to be molded into the players we need to win." The sports writers sat silently as the Bill Burgess era began at Jacksonville State.

My dad often said his goal was to turn young men into great football players and better men. To do this, he had to shape and mold his players, which could be trying for many of them. He couldn't shape and mold them until they understood the order of things. They had to fear, or respect, his authority before he could begin to instill the values of his program.

Dad's plan worked. He coached twelve seasons at JSU, winning four Conference Championships. He went to three National Championships, winning JSU's only National Championship in 1992. He was inducted into the NCAA Division II Hall of Fame, the Gulf South Conference Hall of Fame, the Jacksonville State Athletics Hall of Fame, the Alabama Sports Hall of Fame, the Alabama High School Sports Hall of Fame, and several others. Dad coached sixty-four All-Gulf South Conference players, nine All-Americans, and had numerous players play in the NFL.

These accolades give some indication that Dad's philosophy worked, but they don't compare to the decades of life-change my dad was able to accomplish in his players. I cannot tell you how many men have approached me over the last several decades and asked me if I was Coach Burgess's son. When I proudly reply yes, I am usually told a story of how my dad had been one of the most influential men in their lives. More than one has told me that my dad was the only father they ever had. Several have told me that God had used Dad to save their lives. These are the types of rewards that really matter, the impact we have on other people.

Who is the greatest influence on your life? Who made the most impact on you, specifically as it pertains to your faith? If you have children and asked them this question, how would they respond? Shouldn't it be our goal that they would emphatically answer, "my father"?

It's no coincidence that Dad would build his program upon the foundation of respecting authority. He didn't pull that from thin air. That principle served as the foundation of his faith, which he passed on to us. It's a biblical concept reflected throughout Scripture, but nowhere more simply put than in Proverbs. Proverbs 9:10 says, "The fear of the LORD is the beginning of wisdom, and the knowledge of the Holy One is insight." Proverbs 19:23 says, "The fear of the LORD leads to life, and whoever has it rests satisfied; he will not be visited by harm." Do you hear that, brothers? The fear of the Lord is the foundation from which true transformation flows.

What does it mean to fear God? Does it mean that we approach Him with terror? No. Not at all. The fear we are to approach God with is more of an extreme sense of reverence that comes from understanding who God is and who we are. It is an awe-based respect born out of knowing that God holds every aspect of our lives in His hand, both in this life and the next. It's not a fear as we see in horror movies, but a fear that acknowledges God's majesty, holiness, sovereignty, and, yes, judgment.

A healthy fear of God is the root of a life of character, wisdom, and impact. I remember growing up, hearing the phrase, "God-fearing man." In my world, there was no stronger compliment a man could receive. Do we even use that phrase anymore? I don't hear it very often. It may have gone out of fashion. But the Bible makes it clear that a fear of God is the foundation of a life of real meaning. The man who fears God has wisdom because he is wise enough to fear the wrath and judgment of God. That's the message of Proverbs 19:23. The fear of God helps us avoid all sorts of trouble and brings us peace.

Many people fear God's discipline. But Scripture teaches us that God disciplines those he calls His children out of love for them (Hebrews 12:7–11). When we don't discipline our children, we send them the message that we don't love them enough to correct them. We aren't concerned about the trouble their incorrect behavior will bring them. I can't tell you how many of my dad's former players told me they knew they were loved because my dad, their coach, cared enough about their well-being to teach them to fear authority through discipline.

Never forget that God's barriers are a blessing, not a curse. God is a gracious and merciful God, but He loves us enough to refine us through discipline. Let us be in awe of His authority. Let us be wise by not fearing what we should not fear but making certain that we fear what we should fear: The Great I Am! It's the foundation of God's program to build us up in the likeness of His Son, leveraging our lives for Kingdom impact.

Chapter 10
Can You Go?

My dad's legendary toughness bordered on bizarre. Sometimes, it was as if he didn't experience pain the way people normally experience it. There are so many examples of these moments growing up—too many to list in this book. But one that really sticks out in my mind was the "non-heart attack" he suffered when he was around sixty years old.

At the age of sixty, Dad was very active. He still ran stadiums, exercised regularly, and walked for miles up and down hollows in the great outdoors. Dad was very active but wasn't exactly a health nut regarding nutrition. Like most Southerners, he was raised on what we in the South call soul food. This is the good, southern fare that is prepared with no concern for a calorie count, is often fried, and almost always heavily buttered. When you spend your entire life eating this way, no matter how active you are, it will catch up with you eventually.

When Dad was around sixty, he suffered cardiac arrest at home, and even though this would eventually require a quintuple bypass, until the day he left this earth, Dad claimed that he didn't have a heart attack. My mom described Dad that day as being uncomfortable when he got up, but he still went to work that day and drove himself home, though we would later find out he had to pull over to gather himself before finishing his drive. (And that evening, he also attended a football game he had been invited to.) So, it was somewhat of a surprise to Mom when Dad started feeling ill.

Mom called my brother to come to our parents' home, where he found Dad in pretty bad shape. What actually happened was somewhat of a miracle, or at least divine intervention. Dad had been in the habit of taking ibuprofen pretty much every day of his adult life. The years of football, manual labor, hunting, and fishing had made this a part of his daily routine. This regiment eventually led to Dad having a hole in the lining of his stomach, which was causing him to bleed internally.

We don't know how long this went on, but he never mentioned anything about it to anyone. The doctors later told us that the internal bleeding likely saved his life because it put him (in their medical opinion) in cardiac arrest. If this had not happened as it did, Dad would have continued to ignore his symptoms and likely died in the woods the following hunting season.

So, my dad had a heart attack. Except that he claims he didn't. Why did Dad claim to the day he went to heaven that he did not have a heart attack? Because, according to Dad, he never completely passed out. That was it. That was his rationale. He maintained consciousness, though barely, and because of this, he was sure that no heart attack had occurred. Now, I have consulted doctors and done some Internet research and I have yet to find anywhere that the diagnosis of "heart attack" is only officially declared if the patient completely passes out. But do not tell Coach Bill Burgess that. Because in his mind, it is the only marker that matters.

When the EMTs arrived, they could not get Dad to get on a gurney to be taken to an ambulance. It's important to note that after initial testing, Dad's blood count was measured at eight, which is so low that it is normally cause for a transfusion! Dad is in cardiac arrest (unofficially, of course, because he never fully passed out) and has a blood count of eight but insists on walking to the ambulance. I do not doubt that if he had gotten his way, he would have ridden "shotgun" rather than riding in the back. But thankfully, somehow, my brother finally convinced him to go in the ambulance for our mother's sake, so he did. He would have quintuple bypass surgery and an additional surgery to find the tear in the lining of his stomach. For those keeping score at home, he did officially lose consciousness a few times after the surgeries due to the continued bleeding. Once, he even had to be rushed back to the hospital for a second surgery, but they were finally able to stop the internal bleeding.

Dad made a full recovery. One day, several months after the incident, I sat with him, watching a ball game. Dad asked me if I remembered him passing out and falling into the bathtub while he was in the bathroom. I looked over at him and said, "Yes, Dad. Of course, I remember that. It was frightening, and we were very worried." His reply? "Well, Son, that was your chance to take me. But you missed your opportunity," he said with a sly smile. "I'm at full strength again." I promise you, I thought this was a normal conversation between a dad and his son. I really did.

God put my dad on this earth to be a football coach. There was no doubt about his calling. Dad enjoyed his work, but he also loved to hunt and fish. Most of my memories of Dad do not revolve around football but the great outdoors. In my memories, I harken back to times I found myself walking behind this man of steel, decked out in full camo, walking miles and miles deep into some forest to hunt. And so, it wasn't long after he was cleared for activity that I found myself deer hunting with my dad. As luck would have it, Dad shot a good buck, and before I or anyone else could intervene, I discovered that he had dragged the deer several yards to the dirt road to be picked up in the truck.

I don't know how she found out, but as we were picking Dad up, my mother called me and asked me to tell him that he should not be dragging deer to the road anymore. I did not want to have this conversation with my dad, but Mom clearly instructed me to do so. We returned to the lodge and went to our room to put up our gear. There were two sets of bunk beds, and we had put our gear on the top bunk so we could sleep on the bottom. Dad's back was to me as he put his rifle back in its case on the top bunk. I mustered up the courage to tell him that it really wasn't necessary for him to drag his deer to the road anymore. I pointed out that people were coming to pick us up and could drive the vehicle to the deer. He didn't have anything to prove to himself or anyone else.

I knew it wasn't good when Dad shut the case and turned completely around to face me. The tone in his distinctive baritone voice made me feel like a child again. I was in my forties then but might as well have been eleven. Dad said clearly, "Any man that can't drag his own deer doesn't need to be hunting. You can tell whoever needs to know that I dragged my deer to the road because that is what I do." He then turned back around and finished preparing for the next morning's hunt. I later called my mom and let her know that Dad would continue to drag deer, and if he died with his face in the mud and antlers in his grip, he would die a happy man.

We had a very good team my senior year in high school. We found ourselves in the second round of the playoffs. The playoff system in my home state of Alabama was much different then than it is now. In the eighties, only one team from each area (or region) would make it to the playoffs, meaning you had to win your area. We had teams that would finish nine and one and stay home because the one loss would be to the ten to nothing champion of the area. So, when you hit the playoffs, every team you played was an area champion. There were no easy victories.

It was the second round, and we were facing the number-one ranked team in the entire state for our classification. No one thought we stood a chance against them due to the fact they had destroyed every opponent they had faced. We were a top ten team, but one would be hard-pressed to find a journalist who covered high school football willing to pick us to win. Due to the torrential rain that roared into Alabama that weekend, the game was delayed until Saturday night. The field was still very wet and muddy, which added to the war-like atmosphere of the matchup.

The game lived up to the hype. They were very good, and it was a slugfest from the beginning to the end. We were shocking the world by leading early in the second quarter when something happened to me that had never happened in all my years of playing organized football. I got injured. I wasn't hurt, I was injured. I knew the difference. Anyone who played football knew the difference. Football is a collision (not just contact) sport. It is inevitable that you will get hurt. I had been hurt countless times: a stinger in my shoulder, a broken finger, a sprained ankle, bruises of various kinds, and so on. But this was an injury.

I played defensive tackle, and in that game, I was facing one of the best interior linemen in our state. He would go on to play for the University of Alabama and the Tampa Bay Buccaneers. But that night, I was holding my own against him, good enough, apparently, for his coach to call for a double-team block on me. I wasn't expecting a double team. This guy was so good that he didn't need much help. The double team caught me off guard. Adding a teammate to this human locomotive meant that their combined force driving me off the line of scrimmage was devastating.

I had played defensive line since I was twelve years old, and when I felt the double team, I instinctively knew to drop my shoulder and protect the linebacker. The goal was to stack up the offensive guard and the tackle so the linebacker could make the tackle. The one rule of being double-teamed was to not let them drive you backward. That could not happen. This was ingrained in me by every coach I ever had since I was in the seventh grade. I had stacked up a double-team attempt so many times, but this time was different.

These two had come off the ball so quickly that my right foot got pinned under me when they hit me; it had not yet fully extended out of my initial stance. The force of the two of them was so strong, but then the running back ran into the pile, which only increased the force of the collision. I remember hearing a pop so loud that the most sought-after interior lineman in the State of Alabama said, "What was that sound?" I actually replied from the bottom of the pile, "I think that was my foot breaking." The pain was excruciating. Even still, I fully expected to stand up and walk it off, like I had done many times before. But this time was different. Something was off. The pain was unbearable. But it also just felt unstable. I knew I needed to get to the sideline.

I recall looking back at my teammates on defense. They looked at me as if to say, "Where are you going?" The backup raced past me to fill my spot. Once on the sideline, I sat down and was immediately greeted by the trainer. In those days, we didn't even have a team doctor, much less an orthopedic surgeon. We had coaches, a trainer, and maybe the local chiropractor. I looked at the trainer and told him to tape me up to the point I could at least stand on the foot without it collapsing under my weight. As the trainer taped me, I lifted my head to see my dad approaching. I knew what he was about to ask me.

I had been taught my entire life by the toughest man I had ever known. He had no equal when it came to toughness. He taught his teams to be tough, as well. Year after year, he ingrained into his teams the mindset that if they could be *tougher* than the team across from them, they had a chance to win every game, including games against teams with superior athletes. We had to be able to conquer ourselves before we could ever defeat an opponent. You had to learn not to listen to the voice that says "quit." Sometimes, all you could do was take one more step. And that willingness to dig deep was what separated great teams from good ones.

As Dad approached me, the PA announcer's voice boomed across the field. The band played. The cheerleaders cheered. Our opponent's powerful offense had scored the go-ahead touchdown. Dad locked eyes with me, and I knew exactly what he was about to ask me. It felt like I said yes before he even got the words out. It was as if everything around me got quiet as he looked at me and asked one of life's most important questions: "Hey, can you go?" I stood and faced him like we were the only two men on earth. "Yes, I can go." I turned my face toward the field, buckled my chin strap, and returned to the game. My foot was useless, and I could not play at the same level I had played early in the game. But I was there for my teammates, and that's all they really needed to know.

Did I make any big plays the rest of the game? Not really. I remember being in horrible pain to the point I would squeeze mud through my fingers under the pile just to stand back up. But my teammates played their hearts out, making play after play. And when the final buzzer sounded, we had upset the best team in the state to advance to the next round of the playoffs. You never forget moments like those. They are seared into your memory, still as vivid today as they were forty-plus years ago.

Why was it so important for me to return to the game if I couldn't play at the highest level? Because my teammates needed me. We all had a role to play and I believe they needed to see me in my role, giving it my all and making the opponent account for me. I could not stand on the sideline and expect someone else to do my job. Dad asked if I could go. I could, so I did. I wasn't at my best, but I was in the fight.

When we look at the world around us, especially when it comes to having a spiritual impact, many men are more than willing to stand on the sidelines and are fully willing to let someone else do their job. This is especially true when it comes to them as spiritual leaders in their homes. Many men stand by and watch their wives, a Sunday School teacher, or even a pastor attempt to lead their family spiritually. The only problem with this is that the Bible never names any of these arrangements as viable options.

In Acts 4, we see something very interesting. Peter and John have been radically changed by the resurrection of Christ and the indwelling of the Holy Spirit. These same men ran from difficulty; Peter even denied being associated with Jesus. And yet, after Pentecost, they are willing to suffer for their faith in Christ. They had a boldness they did not have before receiving the Holy Spirit. The Holy Spirit had changed their lives.

We must not forget that we also live on the other side of Pentecost. This means the same power that turned cowardice into boldness is available to all who are redeemed from sin by their faith in Jesus. In Acts 4:13, we see that when those who were persecuting Peter and John saw their boldness, they specifically noted that they had been with Jesus. What was the evidence of their transformation? Their boldness!

The rulers and scribes charged Peter and John not to speak of Jesus anymore, or they would pay a price. And yet, the two men returned to their brothers and sisters in the Jerusalem Church and gathered to pray. What did they pray? That the persecution would stop? No! They prayed for boldness in the face of persecution. They prayed that they would not embarrass Jesus when they were suffering. When they were beaten in Acts 5:38–42, what did they do? Did they complain and say, "Poor pitiful me"? No! They rejoiced that they were worthy enough to suffer for their devotion to Christ.

Peter would later share a similar insight in 1 Peter 1:6–7, where he wrote, "In this you rejoice, though now for a little while, if necessary, you have been grieved by various trials, so that the tested genuineness of your faith—more precious than gold that perishes though it is tested by fire—may be found to result in praise and glory and honor at the revelation of Jesus Christ." Life is hard. Sometimes, we find ourselves dealing with pain that threatens to overwhelm us. It's easy to want to take a play, or a few plays, off. But Peter understands part of why God allows challenges to happen to us in the first place. Peter knows that God is the great refiner.

In this life, we will suffer. But this is how our faith is tested and proven genuine. The next time you find yourself faced with a decision to "stay in the game" or give in to the challenges you face, ask yourself, "Can I go?" And if you have even an ounce of fight left in you, the answer is yes—trust in the power of the Holy Spirit and press on. Look to God and say boldly, "I can go. Put me in."

Chapter 11
Know Where You Are Going

I am sitting in my office while I write this chapter. I am looking at it right now. It sits on a corner of my desk. My mom brought it to me a few months after my dad stepped into the presence of our Lord and Savior, Jesus Christ. It has never been taken out of its original package, but, strangely, it was never returned to the store. It's a Garmin GPS MAP 76.

When I purchased it for my dad, it was the early days of a technology that is now readily available on our phones. These GPS models were larger than our phones and had to be added to the dashboard of your vehicle and put on a charger. They were an exciting and new technology that seemed so futuristic. But in order to fully understand how this GPS ended up in my office, still in its box, all these years later, you have to understand something about my dad.

My dad roamed the never-ending acres of the great outdoors his entire life. It seemed like Dad knew every inch of every dirt road, trail, creek, lake, river, hollow, pasture, and swamp in the

State of Alabama. His love of the outdoors was something that he passed along to his children, especially his two sons. My brother and I can recall so many times that my dad led us into the woods before the sun was even remotely coming up so that we could settle into our spots before the all-day hunt. It's so interesting now to look back as a grown man, with children of my own, and remember being totally at peace walking in darkness along some ridge in the middle of thousands of acres of public land because we were following a man who knew these woods like the back of his hand.

These trips were legendary. Dad would pack our lunches for the day in brown paper sacks, always featuring the same lineup: Ham sandwich, potato chips, one soft drink, and one Little Debbie Nutty Buddy bar. The Nutty Buddy was a Burgess tradition. We had no idea who Little Debbie was with her little straw hat and blue flannel shirt, but her snacks were a staple of our childhood. And the best of the best was The Nutty Buddy.

For the uninitiated, the Nutty Buddy was a couple of wafer cookies stacked with peanut butter on the inside and covered with chocolate. And there were two sticks per pack! Dad always added extra peanut butter by taking a butter knife down the middle of the stacked wafers, spreading Jif peanut butter, and then putting them back together using the peanut butter as the spackle. It took an already delicious treat to the next level. It was snack perfection. I would always try to make the Nutty Buddy bar last, but it never seemed to make it very long.

There were no cell phones in those days, but my dad would give my brother and me walkie-talkies to communicate with each other and him. We also had an empty jug for relieving ourselves if necessary because the one thing you did not do under any circumstances was urinate in the woods while hunting. Unless you wanted every deer in the forest to know you were there. Understand that my brother and I were put up against a tree, sitting on a ridge, and left there all day long. Dad moved on to his spot after dropping us off at our spot. We would sit in the dark until the sun rose and stay there until the sun set again. Again, it's amazing to me to think of how different our childhood was from what passes as normal these days. Most of those days, I didn't take long to eat my sandwich and chips.

There was always a sense of security. I honestly don't recall ever being afraid. Dad seemed to treat this place as if it were his home away from home. As long as he was with us, what could possibly harm us? I felt like Dad could have handled anything we might have encountered in those woods. We had all we needed, and we felt safe.

Hunting was more about the experience than harvesting any animals. When I was a little boy, Alabama didn't have many deer at all. I can only recall seeing a wild deer maybe one time, and I tried to shoot it from about 150 yards with a twenty-gauge shotgun. Dad let me know that was not the best move, but I was thrilled to see one. I preferred rabbit hunting over deer hunting because we were together, had beagles, could talk, and my dad's booming voice could be heard calling and directing the hunting dogs to the next thrilling chase. Deer hunting was all about being quiet, sitting in the woods for hours on end, and usually seeing only a squirrel or two. My brother and I would often get corrected by Dad on the walkie-talkies for talking too much to each other. "Hey, Greg." "Go ahead." "Hey, have you eaten your Nutty Buddy yet?" Dad would break in to remind us that the walkie-talkies were for emergencies or to report a deer sighting, not Little Debbie updates.

It was Father's Day. I don't recall the year, but I know I was now happily married to my wife, Sherri, and we had our own children. My now adult siblings and I usually "unofficially" competed for who could give Dad the best Father's Day present. This was clearly my year. I had found the ultimate gift for Dad. I couldn't wait to shame my brother and sister when Dad opened his new Garmin GPS Map 76. I could imagine his face when he asked me to explain how this brand-new technology that his favorite son had purchased for him worked. He was going to love how much better it made his life.

The moment came after my brother and sister gave him their lame gifts: a book by Louis L'Amour (Dad loved his books), some new hunting gloves, and updated pictures of the grandkids. Not bad, not bad. But I'm sorry, siblings. It's now time to watch the giving of the best gift of the day. I couldn't wait to see Dad's reaction.

Dad picked up my gift and began to open it. I moved in to get the perfect picture of this moment; I was certain he and I would never forget this present. I remember the look on his face when he unwrapped the present and got a look at the box with the picture of this beautiful new technical marvel. Surprisingly, I realized the look was not elation but more like confusion.

Dad looked at me and said, "What is this?" Hoping to explain it to him and finally get the excited reaction I knew would be forthcoming, I replied, "That, Dad, is a GPS. A global positioning system." I was convinced this was my moment. "Dad, this will take you anywhere you want to go. All you do is punch in the address or location; boom, it will take you right to it." I grinned broadly, certain the amazement I expected was sure to follow. I began to imagine us in his Ford Bronco, riding along with his new GPS mounted on the dashboard, him looking over at me to thank me again for his favorite Father's Day gift of all time. But that isn't what happened at all.

Dad looked at me and asked me if I had the receipt. I replied that I did not but asked, "Why would you need the receipt, Dad?" I sensed I was on the verge of disaster. I had to make one more case for my gift. "Dad," I said, "do you realize this GPS will give you directions anywhere you want to go?" I will never forget what he said next.

Dad had a knack for saying things that would render you speechless. He would often say something that would end any further discussion because the statement would be one that left no room for a response. My dad looked at me, looked back at the GPS, and replied, "Rick, I don't ever go anywhere that I don't know how to get there." Another Bill Burgess classic.

I had no response. I watched him put the box next to his chair and continue interacting with his adoring family. I always wondered what had happened to that GPS until Mom found it in his closet not long after his life on Earth had ended. He didn't take it back. He kept it, likely because it was from his son. He

118

never used it because, as he stated, he didn't need it to get where he was going.

In John 14, Jesus has a similar conversation with His disciples. In verses 1–4, Jesus tells them not to be troubled by the trials of a fallen world that would persecute them for their devotion to Him. He reminds them that He is preparing a place for them in His Father's house. Jesus says that He is going and they will be joining Him.

But there is a problem. In verse 4, Jesus told them that He would come for them and show them the way to this place. But Thomas says to Jesus in verse 5 that there is one problem with this location that Jesus spoke of: they don't know how to get there! Jesus replied in verse 6, "I am the way, and the truth and the life. No one comes to the Father except through me."

Do you and I have that kind of faith? Are those words of Jesus enough? Or do you find yourself wanting more details? "Hey, Jesus: what do you mean that you are the way? What address should we punch in to get to heaven?" It doesn't work like that. There is no magical GPS for faith. No, a true saving faith should be us saying to Jesus that His answer is perfect and that we will trust in Him as the way to eternity in the presence of God.

Jesus goes on to discuss directions in Matthew 7 when He discusses two different gates. In verse 13, Jesus tells us that we should enter a narrow gate, for there is another gate that is wide and easy and leads to destruction. He says most people choose the wrong gate.

Why do so many choose the wrong gate? Because the wide way is easy. Sadly, human beings seem to prefer wide and easy because it doesn't require hardship or much attention to navigation. However, there is a problem with this wide and easy gate: its destination is destruction.

Jesus gives the instructions for the correct destination of eternal life. In verse 14, Jesus tells us that this correct destination requires us to enter a narrow gate. This gate isn't so easy to navigate. Jesus says clearly that the way will be hard.

Jesus is saying this way to eternal life is so hard that we cannot expect to navigate it without totally depending on Him. He not only knows the way, He *is* the way. Jesus is the gate and Jesus is the way. To arrive at the destination without following Him step by step is impossible, so impossible that only a few ever enter the gate. Why? Because it requires us to deny ourselves, pick up our cross, and give up our sins.

Sadly, so many of us love our sin so much that we choose the wide gate and the easy way to our own demise. Are you one of the few? Or are you trying to find your way to a location without knowing how to get there? Paul warns the Ephesians in chapter 5 to look carefully how they walk. Verse 15 tells us to walk with wisdom, not like the unwise who have no idea where they are going. Paul goes on in verse 16 and says we should not be foolish on our journey but should understand the will of the Lord. We then find in 1 Thessalonians 4:2 that Paul is encouraging this church that the will of God is our sanctification, which means our holiness.

Jesus is teaching us that in order to find our way, we need to know how to get there. If Jesus is the way to eternal life, then we must know everything about Him. We cannot navigate this difficult journey if we don't know Jesus and His teachings in the Word of God. Maybe it's time for us to stop going down a path of destruction and instead pursue a path of life. The directions are pretty clear. There's really only one way to get there: Follow Jesus.

Chapter 12

What Is a Man?

My dad was always able to get more out of young men than they thought they could accomplish. It's tough to explain how he was able to motivate people to achieve things that, frankly, they should not have been able to do, considering their limitations. Dad was once asked why he did not time his high school players in the forty-yard dash. Dad's unique reply was that he didn't want his players to know how slow they really were. What could possibly be accomplished by confirming that it would take his cornerback a full second longer to run forty yards than the very receivers he would have to cover every Friday night? And yet, Dad consistently got the very best out of his players.

Dad coached high school for most of his coaching career and won many football games with players whom a college team would never recruit. I don't want you, the reader, to think that it was just the fact that he could be hard on his players or just the fear of his authority that made average players do remarkable things. Those things played a role, but it was so much more.

There was something about my dad's persona and his character that motivated people to want to run through a wall for him, not so much because you were afraid to disappoint him, but because you truly loved him. You knew that he always had your back. Over the years, his players have repeatedly used this same phrase: "Coach Burgess was hard, but he was fair."

My dad was put on this earth for many reasons. Undoubtedly, one of God's main callings on his life was to turn boys into men. And he was a master at it. He was a gifted motivator. One of his principles that I have taken to heart is that your rules and standards are the same for everyone, but how you go about getting people to achieve those standards differs from person to person. You cannot motivate different people in the same way. Words that challenge one player may cause a different player to quit. In order to perform at the highest level, some people need challenge, and others need encouragement. Dad knew just what levers to pull to get people to give their best.

One lever that Dad had at his disposal, one that helped sift the potential pool of young men who would experience Dad's impact on their lives, was the game of football itself. Specifically, the physical nature of it. Dad would always remind his players that football is not just a contact sport but a collision sport. There's a difference. Some of the best athletes in the world can't deal with the collision part of the game. I recall such an incident when I was playing high school football for Dad.

Early in the summer, one of our high school track stars came out for the football team. He was a great guy, a gifted athlete, and an exciting new addition. This guy could run for days without seeming to struggle at all. He ran stadiums like they were nothing. Running sprints seemed to bring him joy. The summer workouts were nothing to him, but he had yet to put on the gear and play the game of football. All we knew was that he was very good at track. Then came August.

August in Alabama meant one thing to anyone who ever played football: the dreaded, and now all but outlawed, "two-a-days." When anyone talks with former players who might be missing the thrill of those Friday night lights and asks if they want to play football again, the answer is usually the same: "I would love to play as long as I was able to skip two-a-days." No one in their right mind ever wanted to revisit the hell on earth that was August's two-a-day practice.

To help ease players into the twice-daily practices in the summer heat, the State required three days of practice in shorts, helmets, and shoulder pads. This meant these practices would not be full contact. Dad was no fan of these mandated practices. According to Dad, "Everybody looks good in shorts," which was his way of saying that practicing in shorts didn't give you any idea how someone would handle the contact aspect of the game. But, for our track star, this was the first chance to experience something other than lifting weights and running.

On the first day of summer practice, we suited up in our helmets, shoulder pads, shorts, and cleats for the day's first practice. By all football standards, the practice was very light. It was nothing more than a few "tackling" drills that did not require us to take the other player fully to the ground. The tackler would "lock up" the person running the ball, which means that the defender would lead with his forehand (this was the 1980s), explode into the chest of the person running the ball, wrap their arms around the runner, and then let up. The tackler would then move to the next line to become the ball carrier. These are not violent collisions like a practice in full pads with full-speed blocking and tackling. Those practices were still a few days away.

During the practice, the track star got to run the ball a few times, go through some blocking, and learn the basic points of learning to tackle. By the end of the practice, I began to notice a different spirit in the track star as the practice dragged on. When we got to the sprints that would end the practice, he didn't finish first in his group. He began to lag behind. Dad noticed, which brought the sound of Dad's unmistakable voice cutting across the field. The sound of the eighteen-wheelers that were always passing the field via HWY 78 was no match for Dad's voice. Practice ended, and we shuffled back to the locker room. The track star had experienced a bit of a rough start but had held his own. However, what happened next would decide his future in the game of football.

The distinct smell of dozens of sweaty players filled the air as we filed into the locker room. The track star's locker was next to mine. I remember I had hung up my helmet and was about to remove my shoulder pads when the track star sat on the bench in front of our lockers. He took off his helmet, let out a deep breath, and said, "Man, I hope it's not going to be that rough every day." I stopped dead in my tracks, shoulder pads halfway off. I stared at him for a moment and told him that if he thought today was hard, he would really dislike Thursday! I let him know that today's practice would seem like heaven compared to the physical and mental requirement of Thursday's full pads, full speed, full contact practices.

I watched the wheels spinning as he began to evaluate whether this sport was for him. You see, he did fine when the requirement was running and lifting weights. That little bit of effort, while challenging on some levels, suited him and his talents. But when things got really challenging, when the collisions were introduced, he realized that he had not completely prepared himself for every aspect required to play the game of football. He was not prepared to give what was being asked of him.

He told me that he was going to quit. I told him I understood. Football isn't for everyone. I told him the best thing he could do was not to disappear and never come back; that would only lose the respect of his coaches and teammates. I told him to go to my dad's office and tell my dad that he had concluded that he did not desire to play this game. Look my dad in the eye and turn in your equipment. To his credit, he did just that. He told me that my dad shook his hand, told him that he would be a great asset to our track team, and said he looked forward to seeing him run next spring.

Football doesn't make you a man. Not playing football doesn't mean you're any less of a man. But football has taught an important lesson to countless men throughout the ages, one it still teaches today: you don't really know how you will respond to being hit until you are hit. Some people discover they love contact. Most people tolerate it. Many discover they cannot handle it. The point of this story isn't to imply that anything was lacking in my friend who ran track. The point is that when faced with the demanding challenges of football, he realized he could not rise to the occasion.

In Luke 14:28–33, Jesus tells two parables, one of a man who wants to build a tower and the other of a king who wants to go to war, so we may understand the costs of following Him. He doesn't want any of His followers to be blind to the demands of surrendering to Him. Jesus made it clear that if we repent and decide to follow Him, there will be difficulty. There will be tribulation. There will be collisions with the world and calamities that will test the validity of our faith.

Trials are God's way of both testing and growing our faith. Remember Peter's words in 1 Peter 1:6–7: "In this you rejoice, though now for a little while, if necessary, you have been grieved by various trials, so that the tested genuineness of your faith—more precious than gold that perishes though it is tested by fire—may be found to result in praise and glory and honor at the revelation of Jesus Christ." Don't miss that phrase, "if necessary." God knows what we need in order to prepare us to fulfill our calling. He alone knows when it may be necessary to allow us to go through calamity in order for us to be refined and for Him to be glorified.

Dad had always taught me to be tough. He taught me never to let anyone or anything run over me. He taught me to be a good provider and to stand in the gap for my family to be their protector. He taught me to love my wife and treat her with respect. In short, he taught me to be a man. The type of manhood he passed along to me was following his example of living as if you were indestructible. Burgess men should be the toughest men the world had ever seen. That was the standard. To complain and whine about discomfort or difficulty was unacceptable. You suck it up. You press on. That worked OK until the day God deemed it necessary to refine me: January 19, 2008. The day everything changed.

If you are not familiar with our family's story, I'll bring you into a tragedy that no parent ever imagines they will experience. While I was away speaking at a youth conference in Tennessee, my youngest son, William Bronner Burgess, drowned in our backyard pool. Bronner went to be with his perfect heavenly Father at the age of two and a half years old. My wife Sherri, who is a brilliant writer, unpacked this event and its impact on our lives in her incredibly powerful book *Bronner: A Journey to Understand*. In this book, I will not attempt to add anything to all that God showed Sherri during the five years it took to write her book. I humbly suggest that if you have not read her book yet, do it as soon as you possibly can. In my opinion, it has no equal on the topic of God and suffering. What I am going to do here is share with you the impact this event had on the relationship between my dad and me.

To lose a child is the sort of calamity that is so riveting that it becomes a marker in your life. My life was split in two that day. There is my life before January 19, 2008, and then there is my life since. The two lives are completely different lives. This devastating event made me depend on God like nothing I had ever experienced. Gone was any reliance on my strength, my ability, or my will to continue. I needed God's help to take a step, just to take my next breath. It changed everything I knew about being a husband, a father, and a son. It changed what I thought it meant to be a man.

There are so many ways a loss like that changes a person. One you might not imagine is the freeing sense of the radical perspective change on what really matters. You discover that so much of what you think is important really isn't. I began to understand the depth and the peace of the Apostle Paul's words from a jail cell to the Philippians: "For to me to live is Christ, and to die is gain" (Philippians 1:21). If I were to continue to live, then the only thing that would comfort me was to see this trial glorify Christ. But if the sweet rest and peace of death were to come, then I would know that it would usher me into the presence of the Lord and Savior who redeemed me and my beautiful son. In the years after Bronner's death, I have been heaven-focused and eternity-driven in a way that I never was before.

These lessons, and others, would come later. In the immediate aftermath of Bronner's death, I knew that this horrible tragedy could not be wasted. It had to count for the Kingdom of God. I knew my heavenly Father had something to teach me, and I didn't want to miss any aspect of what He was doing.

One of the many mercies God gave me was a growing spiritual maturity to help minister to and care for my bride, an incredibly powerful woman of God who knows the Scriptures from Genesis to Revelation. Time and time again, God would give me the words to comfort her as she mourned the separation from her child. There were times when I would find her crying on the floor, and she would ask me, again, why this happened. Once, I gently reminded her that she knew the answers, God's character, and why God allows tragedy to strike His children. She replied, with tears streaming down her cheeks, "I know. But tell me again." Nothing shapes a person like grief.

We decided we would have a graveside service just for family. It rained that day. Then, after the graveside, we held a memorial service at our home church and invited anyone who wanted to come. I host a nationally syndicated radio show, and this enabled listeners from all over to be there for the service if they so desired. The plan was for me to thank everyone on behalf of our family, and then our pastor would give a message. The group Casting Crowns was kind enough to come and lead us in worship, including their wonderful song, "Praise You in This Storm."

I remember a huge picture of Bronner on the screen when we walked into the church. It rattled me to my core, and I was nearly overwhelmed with grief. We began to worship the one and only living God through songs of worship and praise. I saw my wife reaching for the heavens as she cried out to her Lord in our time of grief. When it came time for me to speak, I said I wasn't sure I could get up. I recall hearing our pastor inform the overflowing sanctuary that I would say a few words. At that very moment, I felt the supernatural power of the Holy Spirit lift me from the pew and walk me to that stage. I was wholly and completely dependent on God.

I recall thanking everyone and addressing my wife and our four children. I challenged our family that the only way we come out of this is to completely submit ourselves to God and His will for our lives. That was all I was prepared to say. What happened next was unexpected and completely supernatural.

I began to deliver a message God had prepared to speak through me to all who were attending that day and around the world. I did not know it was a message I would deliver. I had not planned on it. I can honestly say that had it not been videoed, I don't know that I would remember what God said through me and what a message He had for people.

The impact was as profound as anything I have had the privilege to be a part of. Hundreds of people repented and decided to follow Jesus because of that message, and that is just those I am aware of. The message was put on this relatively new platform called YouTube, and for about a week was the most viewed YouTube video in the world. There is no way to know how many people God led to Him through the words He gave to me. I know that nearly twenty years later, I still have people come up to me and tell me the impact it had on them. (The service is still on YouTube to this day. It's entitled "A Father's Heart." The link is also at burgessministries.com under "watch.")

Why do I think that message made such an impact? Other than the sovereign will of God, I think it's because people tend to listen more intently to someone who just buried
his two-and-a-half-year-old son. They want to know, in the face of unspeakable loss, if he still loves God and finds hope in this faith that he claimed. They want to know if it's real and if it will stand the test of suffering.

I walked off the platform and returned to my seat next to my wife. I still did not really understand the weight of what had just occurred. Our pastor made the correct call and, under the leading of the Holy Spirit, decided not to follow my message with the planned sermon. He realized what had just happened was God-inspired and sufficient for the moment. He ended the service and dismissed everyone. We were told to go to the fellowship hall, where the church would feed our family and close friends.

As I turned to go up the aisle, people were saying comforting words, putting their hands on our shoulders, or patting our backs. I was more or less in a daze when I heard something that got my attention in a way that few things could.

"Hey! Hey!"

The unmistakable voice of my dad penetrated the cloud of grief, bringing me back to the moment. I knew that voice. I had heard it so many times over my life. That voice had called for my attention. It had given me direction. It had given me support. It had given me correction. It had given me encouragement. I was looking for him. In the fog of the emotions of the day, I had lost track of where he was seated. I heard it again, my head on a swivel to find him.

"Hey!"

I had been hearing the voice of my Heavenly Father so clearly during the last few days. Now, at this moment, I heard my earthly father's voice walking up the aisle toward me. Once more, "Hey," the authoritative tone of a man among men, my dad, and I turned to find the source, the granite-strong face that perfectly fit that voice. There he was, his eyes focused on his oldest son whose heart was broken, not merely hurt but injured, who was trying his hardest to show the world that he was still in the game, he could still go.

Our eyes met above the crowd, maybe thirty feet separating us, and for a moment, we just looked at each other. My dad's eyes went to the floor as if he were trying to gather himself, this mountain of a man, even in his old age. After a brief pause, he raised his head back up, his jaw set. He pointed his massive finger at me and said four words I will never forget as long as I live: "Now, that's a man."

My dad's words would come to mean more to me than I ever imagined they would. Why? Because at that moment, in the valley of the shadow of death, God had corrected how we both defined a man. A *true* man is one who surrenders himself to God. That's really it. Manliness has nothing to do with whether or not you play a sport, pick up heavy things, can physically fight well, catch fish, shoot wild game, climb mountains, or be successful in business. These things can be positive and good but don't make you a man. Dad and I began to realize on that day that real masculinity is humbly coming under the authority of God and obediently following where He leads.

We see this most clearly in the person and life of Jesus. The only perfect example of how to be a man is when God became one. Jesus is our example. He submitted to the Father's will and humbly served, even unto death on the cross. He experienced unimaginable pain and loss. And He did so knowing full well what would be asked of Him. He knew the cost and faithfully carried out the Father's will. In the midst of a great trial, He persevered. He stayed true to His calling and nature. In the end, that is what we are also called to do. Endure under duress with the power of the Holy Spirit to guide us.

As my dad's words washed over me, I nodded back to him and turned to walk out of the sanctuary. In those first days, I was burdened with a weight I didn't know how to carry. I was grief-stricken, overwhelmed, and, if I were totally transparent, I just wanted to leave. I wanted to be anywhere else with my family than in a room full of people. There was a moment, just a moment, where I felt a desire deep within me to run away, to just go. But, with my dad at my back and God's presence with me in a way it had never been before, I squared my shoulders and resolutely walked up the aisle to join my family. After all, men don't run in the rain.

Chapter 13
A True Original

I know we all have heard many times someone described as being "original." We've all heard the phrase, "They broke the mold after God made this one." These descriptions are often exaggerated, but I can say with zero hesitation that Bill Burgess was and is truly one of a kind. This book only scratches the surface when attempting to give the full picture of his uniqueness.

Dad's decade-long battle with Alzheimer's revealed things in him that continued to confirm that he was not like anyone else I know. The first sign that Dad was having issues was the night he got lost in our local wildlife management area. As I have stated, Dad loved the outdoors and knew the thousands of acres of the Choccolocco Management Area as well as anyone. He loved to roam the ridges and hollows looking for deer sign or turkey habitat as he prepared for each hunting season. He was on such a scouting adventure when he got turned around and could not find his way out.

Dad had refused to upgrade his cell phone from the standard flip phone, so he had no GPS. So, instead, he called my brother,

Greg, to let him know that he was lost and could not find his way out of the woods. It was getting dark, and he informed my brother that he was just going to lay down next to a tree, go to sleep, and wait for the sun to come up and walk out the next morning. Well, my brother would have none of that and told Dad that he couldn't just sleep in the woods. We would get in touch with authorities and launch a rescue mission.

Dad knew about Alzheimer's all too well because his dad, my grandfather, had also gotten Alzheimer's, as did all of my grandfather's eleven siblings. Dad had a request for my brother, sister, and me. We had been instructed that if he started to lose his cognitive skills, we were to take him to the woods and leave him so he could live out his final years like some sort of wild man in the forest. I had to inform him that the plan would likely get his children and wife arrested for abandonment. With his wishes in mind, my brother and I wondered if Dad figured out he was slipping and was trying to implement his final plan.

Believe it or not, the rescue team was able to ping that ancient flip phone, eventually finding Dad and bringing him home. This began the horrible journey and battle with Dad's most difficult foe: Alzheimer's. Even during this battle, Dad was still so full of personality and charisma that he won people over wherever we took him. He constantly coached everyone by assuring them they were doing an outstanding job no matter their role at the restaurant, grocery store, doctor's office, pharmacy, etc. It only added to our awe of this man.

Dad eventually lost his short-term memory. His mind would essentially reset every few minutes, and this led to Dad asking lots of the same questions over and over. I watched this man try so hard to fight this horrible disease. He never gave up. He fought it tooth and nail, trying hard to figure out what was happening throughout the day. But even as we lived through my dad's decline, God was merciful in giving us little moments of levity and joy.

Our family has a farm about thirty minutes south of our home in Birmingham, Alabama. God brought this wonderful place of refuge into our lives in the fall of 2007. Sherri and I had no idea God was introducing us to the very place where we would seek refuge to heal after Bronner's death. This place is full of God's presence, and we love to spend time there. My blood pressure drops and I relax the minute my foot touches the grass inside the gate.

As we have established, Dad loved to hunt and fish. One day in the final months of Dad's life, my wife and I took Mom and Dad to the farm to relax. Dad's Alzheimer's was in the later stages then, and he couldn't do much on his own. As we walked around, Dad looked at the pond and asked me how big it was. I replied that it was a little over five acres. (I knew this because it had just been surveyed.) In true Dad fashion, he answered, "Nah, it's bigger than that." He then went on to tell me how he would fish the pond.

Sherri looked at me and told me I needed to take him fishing. My mom quickly warned me that it would break my heart because he couldn't even make toast anymore, and he would likely not remember how to fish. Sherri and I had just watched a documentary about Glenn Campbell and his battle with Alzheimer's. In that documentary, Glenn Campbell was able to remember his songs and how to play guitar to the point that he actually toured with Alzheimer's. The brain is an amazing thing. Apparently, even when Glenn Campbell didn't know what day it was, he could still play his songs. Sherri believed that her father-in-law, or, as she and the grandkids called him, Pop, could likely still fish.

Dad was a wonderful fisherman. I can't tell you the times I would be fishing with him and catch nothing, only to watch him come right behind me with the same lure I was using and catch fish. I once asked him how he could catch fish out of the same hole I could not. His answer? "Presentation, Son, presentation." He also told me that if I ever used plastic worms, I was free to use any color I wanted, as long as it was purple.

So, taking Sherri's advice, I got the rods out and handed Dad one. We were using a lure called a rattle trap. It features multiple treble hooks, making it easy to get hung on structures like limbs or weeds. Dad prided himself on never getting his lures hung, and God forbid you get one hung in his presence. He absolutely hated the thought of a lost lure. It was as if you were fishing with a priceless antique. His tackle box featured lures that were easily 50 years old.

Dad looked down at the rod in his hand for a moment and looked confused. Mom was right; this was going to eat me up. But all of a sudden, the man who didn't know what day or season it was took that open-face reel and tossed a beautiful cast into a perfect spot. He began to reel at the perfect speed, and within just a few seconds, he had a nice largemouth bass on the line. Dad reeled in the fish, took it off the hooks, tossed it back in the water, looked at me, and said, "One to nothing." I looked at Sherri and then at Mom, who rolled her eyes and chuckled under her breath, "Can't even make toast."

As Dad moved around the banks of the pond, I knew he would have forgotten the fish he had just caught and the casts he had just made. I watched as he approached a tree that had fallen in the pond during a storm. If you fish, you know that submerged trees make incredible habitat for fish. But they also represent a place where rattletrap lures go to die! I wondered if Dad would attempt to cast near it.

Dad took one look at those limbs and solemnly warned me to be careful throwing rattle traps around them. "Don't get hung up and lose a lure, Son! Watch what you are doing." I was fifty-eight years old then, but I might as well have been a child at that moment. "OK, Dad," I said as I carefully tossed my lure around the limbs, hoping to land a big one.

As I was reeling my line in, I heard Dad struggling a little. I saw that he had gotten his lure stuck on a tree limb. I walked over and gently asked Dad to give me his rod; I didn't want to embarrass him. He seemed to take it in stride. I insisted he take my rod and keep fishing; the bass were hitting, and I wanted him to enjoy this moment that he would soon forget, but I would remember the rest of my life. That was the most painful shift when Dad got this far along; I knew he would never remember the times we were having together but knew that I would.

So, imagine the picture: My dad has taken my rod and stepped a few feet away to continue fishing. I am trying to get his lure out of the limb. Don't forget that his memory "resets" every few minutes. This is why, a minute or so later, Dad looks up from fishing, sees me struggling with the rod, and says in a very annoyed voice, "Hey! Have you got yourself hung up? What have I always told you? You can't just throw those rattle traps recklessly into those limbs. That's pitiful, Son. And don't break that lure off! I sure hate to lose a lure." Sometimes you just have to laugh.

Instead of being frustrated, I let my mind wander to the many times Dad took me fishing. Alzheimer's was trying to take away a moment, but I wouldn't let it. I decided to enjoy the confusion and let myself be transported to the wonderful childhood this man had given me. "OK, Dad. I'll try not to break off the lure." I then quietly broke off the lure and snuck to the tackle box to put on a new one.

As we walked back to the truck, the sun setting behind us, I suddenly had a memory wash over me. As long as I have known him, Dad drank coffee from the time he woke up until he went to bed. My little brother and I loved to hear him tell us to take the plastic top off his thermos and pour him some black coffee as he drove his beloved Chevy truck or Ford Bronco. Dad had many talents, but driving three on the column while drinking black coffee from a thermos top had to be one of them. I found myself wanting to go to his thermos and, one last time, pour him a cup of coffee like my brother and I did so many times on our various hunting and fishing trips.

Watching the process of how we deal with Alzheimer's patients made it clear to our family that some things in our state had to change. The current process is terribly flawed, but maybe we can be part of bringing some of that change. Things only got worse with Dad. His decline intensified to the point that he became unpredictable, and we put him in memory care. One day, he became aggressive and was sent to the geriatric psych ward in an attempt to find the right drugs to calm him down enough to remain in the memory care community. This was a nightmare. They overmedicated him to the point that when they returned him to memory care, he fell, causing a brain injury that would ultimately take his earthly life.

So it was that we found ourselves all gathered around his bed. A true original was about to leave this earth. Dad was surrounded by the family he loved so much. His wife, whom he loved so dearly, was the center of the universe for Dad. He clung to her when confusion began to rule his days. He had his daughter, whom he had spent a lifetime spoiling (and didn't care who noticed). His grandchildren, who loved their Pop, whom he fawned over so much, giving them anything they wanted, certain that none of them could do any wrong. There were his daughters-in-law whom he loved and bragged about all the time. And his two sons, both of whom hoped they could someday be half the man he was. It was a special time and a fitting "see you soon" to the greatest man I've ever known.

As we watched this legend slip away from this world, my mind replayed a slideshow of him in his prime. One memory stuck with me. Dad is sitting at the helm of my grandparent's old ski boat. Our family would go down to my grandparents' little cabin on the Black Warrior River. It ran all the way to the Gulf of Mexico, and its banks were full of artifacts from the various Native American tribes that had lived there throughout history.

I can still remember my PawPaw, Shorty Burgess, walking with me when I was just a little boy, finding arrowheads all along the banks of that river.

My grandparents had two boat houses, one for PawPaw's fishing boat and one for this old red ski boat. If you were going to MeMaw and PawPaw's river cabin, you had to learn to water ski or face being removed from the family. We had all been dragged behind that ski boat until, wind blowing through our hair, we traveled down that river as if we didn't have a care in the world.

But this vision of Dad isn't a day the boat is pulling skiers. No, we were just cruising down the river as a family. He is driving the boat. Mom is sitting by his side. She is beautiful; wind in her hair, sunglasses on. My little brother, little sister, and I are in the back of the boat. Dad is sitting up on his knees so he can see over the windshield for a better view of the river he loved so much as he drove his family on a sunset cruise. His legs are massive, his arms strong, his profile resolute.

In my memory of that day, the reflection in his sunglasses revealed a coming storm that was all too common on an Alabama summer afternoon. But Dad isn't afraid. He isn't fretting. Even though I was fully aware of the storm, my dad was in charge of the boat, and I felt safe—completely safe, as if the storm should be more afraid of him. We were in no danger because Dad was with us.

I was jolted out of the vision by the conversations in the room that Dad was close to taking his final breath. He had been fighting, typical Bill Burgess. If death was going to shut this body down, it wasn't going to be an easy fight. A doctor had told me earlier in the day that based on everything they saw Dad would not be around much longer. I replied, "You don't know this man; he will not die soon." This was thirteen hours later, and Dad was still hanging on. I wondered why.

Finally, I felt in my spirit that I should tell Dad to go on and let go. I don't know why. I didn't even know if he could hear me. I heard myself saying out loud, "Dad, it's OK. You can go. We are all OK. We will take care of Mom. Your grandchildren and their families are doing well. You got to meet your great-grandchildren! You did your job, Dad. You can go. We will see you soon." It wasn't very long after that that he took one final breath, and his spirit left this world. In the days after his death, my wife would call him our protector. She was so right. I think that is why my mind went to a memory of how safe he made us feel. Men like Dad leave a vacuum when they leave this world. It's up to those of us still here to step in and fill that vacuum.

Dad brought comfort and security to a world that can be a scary place. One of my childhood friends texted me in the days after my dad's death. He was among the many people who saw my dad as a father figure. He said that even when he had not seen my dad in a while, he felt safer just knowing Coach Burgess was alive and walking around. He told me he felt less safe since hearing of my dad's passing. My father followed the example of my heavenly Father, who clearly states that He has not called us to a spirit of fear or to be anxious about anything, but to a spirit of assurance and boldness because we are His children.

Like all true teachers, Dad's lessons flowed without him even trying. Nothing ever felt forced or calculated. And I don't think

Dad understood the fuss over his success or his methods precisely because the lessons he taught were truths he embodied. For him, leveraging his influence was like breathing; it came naturally.

I remember something so clearly during the final days with Dad on this earth. My wife and I love John 16:33 and have clung to it through some of our toughest days. The verse was on a plaque that sat on the entertainment center in Mom and Dad's apartment. Mom and Dad had to move from their house when Dad got to a certain stage to an apartment in a retirement community. Dad was in his final years, and Alzheimer's had taken away most of Dad's ability to carry on a conversation, but he would often see the plaque and remark how much he loved that verse.

Without any warning, Dad would read the verse aloud: "I have said these things to you, that in me you may have peace. In the world you will have tribulation. But take heart; I have overcome the world." He would smile as if to say that though his mind and body were fading, his spirit rejoiced in that truth. He would look at all of us in the room and say, "I like that: 'I have overcome the world.'" Yes, Dad. I like that too. And thanks to Jesus overcoming sin and death, I will get to see you soon. Until then, there will be more work to do.

Epilogue

It's hard to say how thankful I am for the blessing of having an earthly father like Bill Burgess. I continue to hear his voice as I walk through my life. His example drives me, and his instructions flow from me in everything I do. As of the writing of this book, I have not yet had the privilege of being a grandfather, but my grandchildren will know a granddad who is all in, completely invested, and ready to spoil them rotten. Oh, and they will get "the dance." More on this in a moment.

The change I watched as my dad became a grandfather was remarkable but unsurprising. For all my dad's toughness, he was a good person and man. And grandchildren softened him in a way that was amazing to watch. When I have grandkids, I hope to follow my dad's example of being a grandfather. If I am successful at doing so, I will have grandkids who will be allowed to do anything they want at any time, and each will think they are the best at everything they do from their birth to adulthood.

I once asked Dad where my dad was because I did not recognize this man who was now going by "Pop." Who was this man? Was he trying to earn his way to heaven through the treatment of these grandchildren? I wanted to remind him that we are saved by grace, not works.

A great example of this happened on a Tuesday night when one of my sons was playing a little league football game in about the fifth grade. It was the dreaded 7:30 game, usually ending at about 9:15. I was looking for my son when I saw him at the concession stand with this Pop person who had replaced my dad. It's after 9:00 on a school night, and my fifth-grade son is holding a hot dog, nachos, some sort of sour candy, and a soda. I said to Pop, "Dad, why did you get him all that?" To which Dad replied, with a contented grin on his face, "Because that's what he wanted." He then took Mom by the hand, strolled to the parking lot, waved goodbye, and went home, leaving us with a hyper eleven-year-old hopped up on sugar and Coca-Cola. I am almost certain I saw them laughing as they walked.

But about that dance. As I write this, I realize that all my children are adults. When they come to visit my wife and me, we will walk them to the car just like my mom and dad would always walk us to our vehicle. As each child cranks their vehicle to drive away, my wife will say, "Do the dance, do the dance!" and I do the silly little dance just like my dad did for me every time we drove away from his house. I don't know what started it. I don't know exactly why he did it. But every time we would drive away after a family visit, Dad would do this little jig. The grandkids loved it, and we loved it.

I don't know why we loved the little dance so much. Maybe it was because it was such a silly thing for a serious man. But it always made us smile. We would back out of the driveway while this man that so many feared did his silly little dance, seemingly not having a care in the world, so comfortable in his skin, and not taking himself so seriously. He was just joyful and fun; we loved it every time. We would get to the end of the driveway, and when the automobile faced forward to leave, I would always get one more look at the man I loved and admired still committed to the dance as we drove away. I do the dance for my children, and if I am blessed to have grandkids, I pray they get to see it, too.

I am so thankful that, unlike so many, my dad told me often that he loved me. He always told me how proud he was of me. He spent time with me. He encouraged me. He valued me and cared enough for me to not only care for me but to discipline me. I don't have the baggage so many people have when it comes to my relationship with my dad. But I know many of you reading this book are less fortunate.

My dad was not perfect, but he was a good husband to my mother and a good father to his children. The regrets I have in my life are not because of the failures of my mother or father; they were my fault for not listening to their teachings. I know that is a blessing because, sadly, so many times there are terrible wounds caused by earthly fathers who do horrible things or just don't handle their role as husband and father very well. It causes a lot of hurt, and I am not overlooking its impact.

I can't tell you how many times someone has asked me how they are supposed to follow God's instructions to honor their mother and father. I hear them say that they do not like their parents or their father due to the things they did or did not do. If this describes you, I want to focus on the commandment itself for a moment to help you clarify God's command to honor your parents.

The fifth commandment says, "Honor your father and your mother, that your days may be long in the land that the LORD your God is giving you" (Exodus 20:12). You may have heard it taught that this is the first commandment with a promise: Honor your parents so that it may go well with you. That sounds pretty important, as if God is reminding us that if we want to be in the right relationship with Him, this is something we must do.

Jesus drives home the commandment in the New Testament when He calls out the Pharisees and scribes who are questioning His disciple's behavior concerning washing their hands when they eat. Jesus points to the sin in their own life by reminding them that they are breaking the commandment by not honoring their father and mother (Matthew 15:4–7).

In Chapter 19, Matthew records another moment during a conversation with the rich young ruler who asks Jesus what good deed he must do to have eternal life. Jesus tells him to keep the commandments. When Jesus is asked to tell him which ones he should keep, we see Jesus remind him to honor his father and mother. This must be a big deal to God.

And yet some of you reading this are saying, maybe even out loud, "Rick, you don't know what my dad did! You don't know how I was treated! Rick, your dad sounds great, but I did not have a Bill Burgess." I get it, and you are right; I did not live what you lived. But I do understand the dilemma. Let me try to help.

Focus on what the commandment says and what it doesn't say. The commandment very specifically says to "honor" your father and your mother. *Honor* them. It doesn't say like them. It doesn't say condone their actions. It doesn't even say to love them. It says to honor them. What does this mean exactly?

The commandment to honor our parents means that you and I should live our lives in such a way that when people know that they are our parents, it brings honor to them, whether we think they deserve it or not. It's a commandment for how we should live our lives, not a commentary on how they lived theirs. We live a life that brings honor to our heavenly Father in such a way that it also brings honor to our earthly father.

If your dad was a terrible husband, then be a great husband. If your dad was a terrible daddy, then be a great daddy. If your dad was a joke as a grandfather, then be the best grandfather your grandchildren have ever seen. If your dad left, don't leave. If your dad was violent, then be gentle. If your dad was absent, be present. Be an honorable man. If your dad didn't follow Jesus and lead his family to the foot of the cross, then repent, confess Jesus as Lord, bathe your family in prayer and the Word of God, and lead them to the foot of the cross. You be the spiritual leader he never was. Finally, forgive your dad. This doesn't mean that what he did was OK or didn't matter. It just means you love Jesus enough not to deny the grace and forgiveness to your dad that Jesus so freely gives you.

Bitterness is only hurting you. Let it go. Satan will use it against you. You can't control how your dad lives his life, but you can control how you live yours. Live a life that brings him honor whether he deserves it or not because that's what God commanded.

There's one final story that I wanted to include in this reflection on my dad. This seems like a fitting place for it. I was coaching one of my sons in a ballgame, and my son took an illegal shot from a defender and went down on the field. As I left the sideline going onto the field, I said something to the opposing coach about the cheap shot and getting his players under control. I didn't yell or use profanity. I simply said what I said. The opposing coach went off, giving me a piece of his mind and threatening to fight me.

I ignored this as I was going further out on the field to check on my son. As I was on the field, I heard another man from the stands screaming my name, threatening me as well, and even telling me that he hated my radio show. (Of course, everyone is entitled to their opinion, but I found his choice of venues to vent his dislike of my show interesting. Oh, well. To each his own.) I looked at the official and told him to control this thing, or we would have a scene. Things calmed down, but as I bent down to tend to my son, I heard the man in the stands scream loudly that he would be waiting for me in the parking lot.

My son was fine, the game ended, and as I walked off the field, my wife got to me first and wisely instructed me to go straight to my truck and not engage this man. "You have too much to lose and nothing to gain," she said. She was right, of course.

I had ridden separately from my wife because I needed to get to the field early. Mom and Dad were there, as well, as they were always supportive of their grandchildren, just as they had been for their own children. As I was walking to the parking lot, I saw my mother, but I did not see Dad. I was telling Mom goodbye as I tried to keep in mind my wife's instructions not to delay. But I was curious. "Mom," I asked, "where is Dad?" "Oh," she said. "He's got popcorn, and he's in the parking lot to see if you are going to fight." And that's Dad. In his seventies, he had my back. Nothing would keep him from protecting those God had entrusted to him.

I am sixty years old as I am writing this. I can honestly say I feel stronger now than I did twenty years ago. Research has shown that if a man still has his mental and physical health, the most impactful decade of his life is from age sixty to seventy. I am embarking on a new journey with my radio career and am excited about all God has planned for my wife and me through the ongoing ministry opportunities that are before us.

Dad has passed on from this earth, but his presence will live on through all those, including me, that he influenced. I don't know whether the Lord allows Dad to see from heaven, but as I face the next phase of my life with all the battles that are still in front of me, I am working to not be anxious about anything. I am endeavoring to live with a spirit of boldness and not fear. I am striving to finish the race. I better, because if Dad's eyes are on me, I just know that he will still be curious to see if, faced with life's challenges, I will fight or not. I would expect nothing less from him.

Chapter Questions

Chapter 1

1. What "past victories" or spiritual milestones do you find yourself dwelling on, and how can you ensure they don't prevent you from seeking new growth in your faith?

2. How might God be calling you to step out in faith today rather than resting on what you've done before?

3. In what ways are you intentionally pursuing spiritual growth and obedience to God in your current season of life?

4. Philip continually obeyed the Spirit's leading. How can you remain attentive to the Holy Spirit's guidance in your daily life?

5. Reflect on Proverbs 27:2. How do you guard against becoming an "empty wagon" in your spiritual walk, making noise without substance?

Chapter 2

1. What challenges or trials in your life have made you want to step back or give up on your faith? How can Paul's example of enduring "forty lashes less one" inspire you to persevere?

2. Bill Burgess' mantra, "You can't worry about that," emphasizes focusing on the goal rather than the hardship. How can adopting this mindset transform the way you approach spiritual struggles or setbacks?

3. Paul considered everything he endured "rubbish" compared to gaining Christ. What in your life might you be holding onto that prevents you from fully committing to Christ? How can you begin to let go of it today?

4. Think about the "fire ant moments" in your life, those times when discomfort or pain tested your faith. How did you respond, and what can you learn from those experiences to better handle future challenges?

5. Paul's unwavering devotion to the Gospel inspires boldness. Are there areas where fear or discomfort has held you back from living out your faith publicly? What specific steps can you take to overcome these barriers?

6. Scripture repeatedly calls us to focus on the eternal rather than the temporary. How can you adjust your daily habits and mindset to prioritize Christ's mission over the distractions or discomforts of life?

Chapter 3

1. Proverbs 12:1 states, "Whoever loves discipline loves knowledge." How do you currently respond to correction or discipline in your life? What steps can you take to view God's discipline as an act of love rather than punishment?

2. Are there areas in your life where you are playing "daredevil" with sin? How can you cultivate a heart that turns away from sin and seeks godly wisdom instead?

3. How well do you control your temper and emotions when provoked? What practices can help you grow in patience and self-control?

4. Proverbs 28:26 advises against relying solely on one's own understanding. How often do you seek God's guidance in making decisions? In what ways can you actively trust God's wisdom over your own instincts?

5. The chapter emphasizes the ultimate foolishness of believing you can earn God's approval through your own efforts. Have you surrendered your life to Jesus, and how does this impact your daily decisions and actions?

Chapter 4

1. In what areas of your life are you tempted to take control and "do things your way" instead of trusting in God's plan and timing? How can you practice surrendering your will to align with God's will in those areas?

2. This chapter discusses people who claim to act in Jesus' name but are actually seeking to glorify themselves. How do you keep your motives pure and centered on glorifying God rather than yourself?

3. When faced with challenges, how do you maintain humility to seek God's guidance rather than relying on your own wisdom?

4. Jesus speaks about those who call Him "Lord" but are not truly in a relationship with Him. How would you describe your current relationship with Jesus? What practices can you implement to deepen your relationship with Him and ensure it's based on genuine faith?

5. Reflecting on the phrase "my way or the highway," are there aspects of your life where you've resisted submitting to God's authority? What steps can you take to fully trust in God's leadership in those areas?

6. What role do Scripture and prayer play in keeping you on the path of true obedience?

Chapter 5

1. Are there areas in your life where you are content to remain a spectator rather than fully committing to being a participant? What steps can you take to "get out of the stands" in your walk with Christ?

2. Paul's obedience stemmed from gratitude for his redemption. How can you cultivate a deeper sense of gratitude for what Christ has done for you, and how can that gratitude shape your daily choices and actions?

3. Do you prioritize the applause and approval of the world over the "well done" from your Heavenly Father? What practical changes can you make to ensure your life is focused on pleasing God?

4. How might past spiritual successes or failures be holding you back from striving for growth today? What does it look like for you to "forget what lies behind" and "press on" toward what God has for you?

5. Paul obeyed out of love for Christ, not to earn salvation. What motivates your obedience to God? How can you shift your perspective to see obedience as an act of love and worship rather than duty?

Chapter 6

1. Reflect on a recent situation where you made a mistake. Did you take full ownership, or did you find yourself making excuses? How can you cultivate a habit of owning your failures and learning from them?

2. How do you understand the concept of repentance as a 180-degree turn from sin? What steps can you take to practice true repentance in your daily life?

3. The chapter highlights the importance of leading by example. Are there areas in your leadership (at work, home, or church) where you need to align your actions more closely with the standards you expect from others?

4. How does Jesus' call to repentance challenge the way you view your sin and need for change? How can you respond to this call more fully in your life?

5. Consider areas where you may be justifying sin or spiritual complacency. What steps can you take today to stop making excuses and pursue a deeper, more authentic relationship with Christ?

Chapter 7

1. Can you think of a recent situation where you might have crossed the line from confidence into arrogance, and how could humility have shaped your response differently?

2. In what areas of your life can you lead by example, as Jesus and Coach Burgess did? Are there any tasks or responsibilities you currently avoid that you could embrace to demonstrate humility and servant leadership?

3. How do you ensure that the gifts and talents God has given you are used to glorify Him rather than to promote yourself? Are there any areas where you need to refocus your efforts to ensure God is receiving the credit?

4. How do you respond to challenges or "thorns" in your life that keep you humble? Do you view them as obstacles, or

do you see them as opportunities for God's power to be made perfect in your weakness?

5. Paul embraced his weaknesses so that Christ's power could rest upon him. In what areas of your life might you need to stop hiding or denying weaknesses and instead allow God to use them for His glory? How can you trust God more in those areas?

Chapter 8

1. How does striving for perfection in your life or faith mirror or differ from the concept of perfection as described in the chapter? Are there areas where you are relying on your own efforts instead of relying on Jesus' sacrifice to make you righteous?

2. Consider Bill Burgess's example of allowing his players to hold him accountable. How can you create structures of accountability in your own life to help you grow in areas where you struggle?

3. This chapter highlights both giving and receiving correction with grace. How do you typically respond when someone points out areas of growth in your life? What steps can you take to better accept constructive criticism as a path to improvement?

4. The chapter explains the roles of justification and sanctification in the Christian life. How are you actively participating in the sanctification process? Are there spiritual

disciplines you could adopt or strengthen to abide more fully in Jesus?

5. How does the idea that perfection is the standard, yet unattainable without Jesus, challenge or comfort you? How can you rest in the assurance of Jesus' righteousness while still pursuing growth in your faith?

Chapter 9

1. How do you respond to authority in your life? Are there areas where you resist or struggle with it, and how can you work towards a healthier respect for authority?

2. Coach Burgess demonstrated his love for his players through discipline. Reflect on a time when you received discipline that shaped your character. How can you view discipline from God or others as an expression of love?

3. What does it mean for you to fear God in a reverent way? How does this fear influence your daily decisions and actions?

4. Coach Burgess aimed to shape his players into better men and athletes through correction and accountability. How are you allowing correction and accountability to shape your character today? Are you inviting others to hold you accountable?

5. If you are a parent, are you intentionally shaping your children's character and faith? If not, who are the key

influencers in your life, and how can you emulate their positive traits?

6. Scripture teaches that God disciplines those He loves. How have you experienced God's discipline in your life? What lessons have you learned from those experiences, and how have they helped you grow closer to Him?

Chapter 10

1. Reflect on a time when you were tempted to step back but chose to press on. How did that decision impact you and others around you?

2. Consider Peter's teaching in 1 Peter 1:6–7. How might trials in your life be refining your faith or character?

3. In what ways do you rely on the power of the Holy Spirit to face life's difficulties? How can you demonstrate boldness in your faith like Peter and John did?

4. When faced with the question, "Can you go?" in your faith or life responsibilities, how do you typically respond? What would it look like to say, "Yes, I can go," even when you're not at full strength?

5. How do you support and encourage others who are struggling to stay in the fight? Reflect on how your actions and attitudes can inspire perseverance in those around you.

Chapter 11

1. Jesus speaks of the narrow gate that leads to life and the wide gate that leads to destruction. What choices in your daily life align with walking through the narrow gate? Are there areas where you are choosing the easier, wider path, and how can you shift your focus?

2. Thomas expressed uncertainty about knowing the way to the destination Jesus described. Are there aspects of your faith journey where you feel unsure or lack clarity? How can you lean on Jesus rather than seeking worldly solutions?

3. The narrow path requires self-denial, carrying one's cross, and turning from sin. What specific sins or self-centered habits might you need to surrender to fully follow Jesus?

4. How intentional are you about studying God's Word and growing in relationship with Him? What steps can you take this week to deepen your understanding and connection?

5. Paul calls believers to walk in wisdom and understand the will of the Lord. How do you discern God's will for your life? Are there practical ways you can prioritize holiness and wisdom in your daily walk?

6. The chapter highlights the power of knowing and following Jesus in leading others to life. How can your faith and actions help guide someone else who may be lost or unsure

of their path? Who in your life might need encouragement to follow the narrow way?

Chapter 12

1. How do you currently define manhood or adulthood in your life? Reflect on whether your definition aligns more with societal expectations or the biblical example of surrendering to God's authority, as shown by Jesus.

2. How do you respond when faced with a situation that tests your faith or character? Think about a recent trial and evaluate whether your response reflected trust in God's plan and the power of the Holy Spirit.

3. What legacy are you building for your family or those you influence? Reflect on whether your actions and character inspire others to rely on God, as the narrator's father did.

4. How does the example of Jesus' obedience to the Father's will challenge your approach to life's difficulties? Reflect on how Jesus' humility and endurance can guide you in living out your calling with faithfulness.

5. What does enduring under duress with the help of the Holy Spirit look like in your current circumstances? Think about how you can actively depend on God's strength to navigate challenges instead of relying solely on your own abilities.

Chapter 13

1. Coach Burgess brought comfort and a sense of security to those around him, even in his final days. Who has made

you feel secure in times of fear or uncertainty? How can you embody that sense of assurance for others, especially in your family or community?

2. Coach Burgess taught life lessons effortlessly by living out his values. What are the key truths or principles you hope to pass on to others? Are you living in a way that naturally reflects those truths?

3. The plaque with John 16:33 reminded Coach Burgess of peace and victory through Christ, even as his body and mind failed him. How does your faith sustain you during trials? How can you remind yourself daily of God's promises and Christ's victory?

4. Coach Burgess left a "vacuum" that others needed to fill after his passing. Are there areas in your family, church, or community where a leader or figure of strength is needed? How can you step into those roles and provide guidance, comfort, or stability?

5. Jesus promised peace even amidst tribulation. What practical steps can you take to lean into God's peace during your own struggles, and how can you help others do the same?

Acknowledgments

This book is written in honor of my dad, Bill Burgess, a true original.

I must first thank my Lord and Savior, Jesus Christ, who, by His grace and mercy, redeemed me and is sanctifying me each day. My only hope is to live in such a way to bring you glory and advance your Kingdom.

I must say thank you to my beautiful, godly wife, Sherri. You are such a gift to me. Thank you for inspiring me, teaching me, encouraging me, defending me, and loving me. God used you to save my life. To Brandi, Blake, Brooks, Brody, and Bronner: thank you, children. What gifts you are from God. Mom, I thank you for not giving up on me when I was far away from God and for the many prayers you prayed for me. Thank you for being a great wife and mother. Greg, I love you brother. Thank you for always being there for me. Lisa, thank you for always having my back, sister. To Angey: I love you, sister, and I am so proud of you.

To my friend Rich Wingo: thank you for holding me accountable. Mark Garnett, Jordy Henson, and Scott Dawson, thank you, men, for discipling me and being such great friends. Danny

Wood, thank you for pastoring my family through tough times and growing us and our faith. To Calvin "Speedy" Wilburn: I can't believe we are still on the air together. Here's to many more years. Chris Adler, thank you for your incredible support and all the content you have helped me produce. It matters greatly. To Bill Bussey: thank you for thirty-one years of *The Rick and Bubba Show*; it was a blast. Ken "Bones "Hearn, thank you for your servant's heart. To "Team Man Church" and Iron Hill Press, Les Bradford, and Andy Blanks: thank you for trusting me enough to publish my work. Working with you two is a pleasure. To Summit Broadcasting: thank you for partnering with and believing in *The Rick Burgess Show*. And last but definitely not least, to SSI and Bob Carey: Thank you for taking the show across the nation.

About the Author

Rick Burgess

Rick Burgess is the host of the nationally syndicated radio show, *The Rick Burgess Show*. (He previously co-hosted *The Rick and Bubba Show* for thirty-one years). He has authored "Sin Always Matters: The Cost of Sin and the Power of Grace" and "Transformed: Embracing the Death of Self and the Power of God," as well as co-authoring multiple New York Times bestselling books and the "How to Be a Man" series of devotionals. As a commentator and guest, Rick has appeared on various radio and television shows, including Fox and Friends and the Sean Hannity Show. Rick is a frequent speaker at church services and marriage conferences, but his true passion is men's ministry. As founder of "The Man Church" (themanchurch.com), Rick calls on the modern church to put into practice what they say every Father's Day, that a man's family will follow him if he leads them.

Rick and his wife Sherri were married in 1996, have five children, and reside in Birmingham, Alabama. Rick's Spirit-filled message at their youngest son's memorial service was the most-watched video on YouTube in the world the week it was posted. Find out more about their ministry by going to burgessministries.com.

Equipping the Church to know God
through His Word.

ironhillpress.com   800.307.9366